OPPOSING VIEWPOINTS® SERIES

Criminal Justice

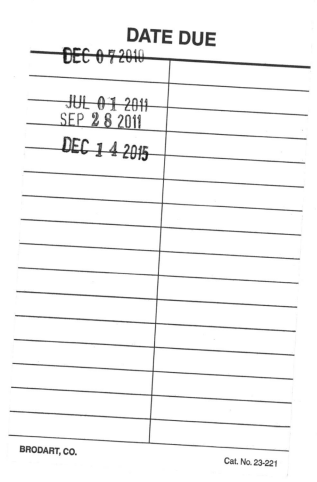

Other Books of Related Interest:

Opposing Viewpoints Series
Police Brutality

Legal System

Current Controversies Series
Capital Punishment

At Issue Series
Does Capital Punishment Deter Crime?

Racial Profiling

"Congress shall make
no law . . . abridging
the freedom of speech,
or of the press."

First Amendment to the U.S. Constitution

The basic foundation of our democracy is the First Amendment guarantee of freedom of expression. The *Opposing Viewpoints* Series is dedicated to the concept of this basic freedom and the idea that it is more important to practice it than to enshrine it.

OPPOSING
VIEWPOINTS®
SERIES

Criminal Justice

David Haugen and Susan Musser, Book Editors

GREENHAVEN PRESS
A part of Gale, Cengage Learning

GALE
CENGAGE Learning™

Detroit • New York • San Francisco • New Haven, Conn • Waterville, Maine • London

Christine Nasso, *Publisher*
Elizabeth Des Chenes, *Managing Editor*

© 2009 Greenhaven Press, a part of Gale, Cengage Learning

Gale and Greenhaven Press are registered trademarks used herein under license.

For more information, contact:
Greenhaven Press
27500 Drake Rd.
Farmington Hills, MI 48331-3535
Or you can visit our Internet site at gale.cengage.com

For product information and technology assistance, contact us at

Gale Customer Support, 1-800-877-4253
For permission to use material from this text or product, submit all requests online at
www.cengage.com/permissions

Further permissions questions can be emailed to permissionrequest@cengage.com

Articles in Greenhaven Press anthologies are often edited for length to meet page requirements. In addition, original titles of these works are changed to clearly present the main thesis and to explicitly indicate the author's opinion. Every effort is made to ensure that Greenhaven Press accurately reflects the original intent of the authors. Every effort has been made to trace the owners of copyrighted material.

Cover image © Victoria Alexandrova Dreamstime.com

LIBRARY OF CONGRESS CATALOGING-IN-PUBLICATION DATA

Criminal justice / David Haugen and Susan Musser, book editors.
    p. cm. -- (Opposing viewpoints)
Includes bibliographical references and index.
ISBN 978-0-7377-4198-8 (hardcover)
ISBN 978-0-7377-4199-5 (pbk.)
1. Criminal justice, Administration of--United States. I. Haugen, David M., 1969-
II. Musser, Susan.
HV8141.C67 2009
364.973--dc22

                                       2008030545

Printed in the United States of America
2 3 4 5 6   14 13 12 11 10

ED131

Contents

Chapter 3: Should Sentencing Laws Be Reformed?

Chapter 4: Are Defendants' Rights Protected in the United States?

Why Consider
Opposing Viewpoints?

> *"The only way in which a human being can make some approach to knowing the whole of a subject is by hearing what can be said about it by persons of every variety of opinion and studying all modes in which it can be looked at by every character of mind. No wise man ever acquired his wisdom in any mode but this."*
>
> John Stuart Mill

In our media-intensive culture it is not difficult to find differing opinions. Thousands of newspapers and magazines and dozens of radio and television talk shows resound with differing points of view. The difficulty lies in deciding which opinion to agree with and which "experts" seem the most credible. The more inundated we become with differing opinions and claims, the more essential it is to hone critical reading and thinking skills to evaluate these ideas. *Opposing Viewpoints* books address this problem directly by presenting stimulating debates that can be used to enhance and teach these skills. The varied opinions contained in each book examine many different aspects of a single issue. While examining these conveniently edited opposing views, readers can develop critical thinking skills such as the ability to compare and contrast authors' credibility, facts, argumentation styles, use of persuasive techniques, and other stylistic tools. In short, the *Opposing Viewpoints* series is an ideal way to attain the higher-level thinking and reading skills so essential in a culture of diverse and contradictory opinions.

In addition to providing a tool for critical thinking, *Opposing Viewpoints* books challenge readers to question their own strongly held opinions and assumptions. Most people form their opinions on the basis of upbringing, peer pressure, and personal, cultural, or professional bias. By reading carefully balanced opposing views, readers must directly confront new ideas as well as the opinions of those with whom they disagree. This is not to simplistically argue that everyone who reads opposing views will—or should—change his or her opinion. Instead, the series enhances readers' understanding of their own views by encouraging confrontation with opposing ideas. Careful examination of others' views can lead to the readers' understanding of the logical inconsistencies in their own opinions, perspective on why they hold an opinion, and the consideration of the possibility that their opinion requires further evaluation.

Evaluating Other Opinions

To ensure that this type of examination occurs, *Opposing Viewpoints* books present all types of opinions. Prominent spokespeople on different sides of each issue as well as well-known professionals from many disciplines challenge the reader. An additional goal of the series is to provide a forum for other, less known, or even unpopular viewpoints. The opinion of an ordinary person who has had to make the decision to cut off life support from a terminally ill relative, for example, may be just as valuable and provide just as much insight as a medical ethicist's professional opinion. The editors have two additional purposes in including these less known views. One, the editors encourage readers to respect others' opinions—even when not enhanced by professional credibility. It is only by reading or listening to and objectively evaluating others' ideas that one can determine whether they are worthy of consideration. Two, the inclusion of such viewpoints encourages the important critical thinking skill of objectively evaluating an author's credentials and bias. This evaluation will illuminate an author's reasons for taking a particular stance on an issue and will aid in readers' evaluation of the author's ideas.

It is our hope that these books will give readers a deeper understanding of the issues debated and an appreciation of the complexity of even seemingly simple issues when good and honest people disagree. This awareness is particularly important in a democratic society such as ours in which people enter into public debate to determine the common good. Those with whom one disagrees should not be regarded as enemies but rather as people whose views deserve careful examination and may shed light on one's own.

Thomas Jefferson once said that "difference of opinion leads to inquiry, and inquiry to truth." Jefferson, a broadly educated man, argued that "if a nation expects to be ignorant and free . . . it expects what never was and never will be." As individuals and as a nation, it is imperative that we consider the opinions of others and examine them with skill and discernment. The *Opposing Viewpoints* series is intended to help readers achieve this goal.

David L. Bender and Bruno Leone,
Founders

Introduction

> *"Although Americans only constitute 5 percent of the world's population, one-quarter of the entire world's inmates are contained in our jails and prisons, something that baffles other democratic societies that have typically used prisons as a measure of last resort, especially for nonviolent offenders." —Silja J.A. Talvi,* The Nation, *January 2007.*

> *"We should not celebrate the fact that America's prisons are so full, but on balance it's not such a bad thing—provided they're full of criminals." —Robert E. Moffit and David B. Muhlhausen,* Human Events, *July 2000.*

The criminal justice system in the United States is composed primarily of the police, the courts, and the correctional programs and facilities. Together these elements have the purpose of deterring and controlling crime throughout the nation. Ideally each part of the criminal justice system is expected to carry out its duties fairly, impartially, and with the highest regard for justice. In the country's courts, for example, this means that all defendants are presumed innocent until proven guilty and that any resulting sentences handed down to those proven guilty reflect the laws of the land and the seriousness of the crimes committed. Whether such impartiality is maintained in the courts or any other part of the criminal justice system, however, is the subject of controversy. Critics of the system allege that there are failings at all levels, pointing out that mostly poor and minority Americans have become the unfortunate victims of police profiling, inadequate legal defense, and harsher court sentencing coupled with lengthy incarceration.

Though the accuracy of these charges is disputed, the criminal justice process has left America with the highest incarceration rate in the entire world. In 2006, the Department of Justice reported that one in every 32 adults is under some form of correctional supervision—meaning that roughly 7 million people are in jail or prison, on parole, or serving probationary sentences. Some say this is a sad commentary on American society and not an indictment of the system, but many legislators are looking for ways to reform the criminal justice system to change the nation's image and to alleviate the problems that attend high prison populations.

In a 2008 issue of *Policy Today* (a California-based e-magazine that addresses a wide-range of social and political issues), freelance journalist Howard Unger describes how some state legislatures are coping with high incarceration rates. Unger reports that Massachusetts has so many nonviolent criminals behind bars that the state spends more on prisons than on higher education programs at its well-known and well-respected universities. Similarly, according to Unger, the state of Texas is looking at ways to reduce prison overcrowding by rethinking the way its courts treat nonviolent offenders. Lawmakers in both states are turning their attention to rehabilitation and treatment programs, especially for individuals convicted of drug-related crimes. Unger quotes Texas state senator John Whitmire as stating, "We're tough on violent offenders in Texas. We've got to get smart on non-violent offenders." Whitmire and his supporters oppose a blanket policy that simply seeks to "lock everybody up."

Whitmire's ally is Texas House of Representatives member Jerry Madden. Madden is the author of Texas House Bill 530, a law that would expand the use of drug courts to deal with nonviolent addicts. The law was in part a reaction to news that Texas taxpayers might be required to offer up $420 million to construct three new prisons, which would cost another $600 million to operate over ten years. Madden's bill overwhelmingly passed the Texas House and Senate in spring 2007 and was signed into law by Governor Rick Perry. "People have recognized that the alternative to diversionary programs is to keep building prisons forever," Madden said.

Rehabilitation and treatment programs are growing in popularity given the rising costs of incarceration. According to the Federal Bureau of Prisons, it costs taxpayers over $23,000 dollars per year to house each federal prison inmate (and over $20,000 for prisoners housed in state facilities). These figures pushed federal and state lawmakers to incorporate drug treatment programs in many prison facilities and it also prompted the creation of specific drug courts in the late 1980s to deal with people whose major crime was their drug dependency. According to the Office of National Drug Control Policy (ONDCP), there are more than 2,100 drug courts across the United States. These institutions offer convicts treatment options and probationary supervision in lieu of jail time. ONDCP maintains that research has shown these courts to be an economical alternative to incarceration.

Together drug courts and drug treatment programs in prisons have reportedly fulfilled their promise by reducing recidivism rates (i.e., re-arrest rates). In 2005, the Center for Court Innovation, a New York state and city nonprofit that tries to find solutions for justice-system problems, cited evidence that recidivism in drug court cases was on average 13 percentage points lower than comparable cases that went through traditional courts (which have a recidivism rate of 50 percent). Unger says that Idaho has become a model of rehabilitation and treatment, showing recidivism rates of 33 percent, and other states are taking notice in hopes of avoiding bigger prison budgets.

Some analysts claim that the majority of prisons never see such a return on their rehabilitation investment. Furthermore, those critics who believe that imprisonment is a deterrent to crime reject rosy notions that keeping convicts out of prison is the appropriate solution. Dan Seligman, writing in *Forbes* magazine, argues that it is wrong to paint nonviolent drug offenders as harmless victims of the prison system:

> The "nonviolent" prison population is indeed sizable, but it isn't harmless. [In 2004] the Justice Department's statistical bureau turned in a group portrait of inmates who were about to be released after serving time for nonviolent offenses. The data tell us that 95% had an arrest history before the arrest that led to their current imprisonment. On average they had 9.3 prior arrests and about a third of these had been for violent crimes. The fact is that a sizable proportion of criminals sentenced for nonviolent offenses like buying dope is, in fact, chronically violent.

Seligman is concerned about the high recidivism rate of all convicts and believes that imprisonment assures society that offenders will not be on the streets. While Seligman does not disparage rehabilitation programs, he maintains that the nation's declining crime rates are due to the fact that criminals of all stripes are behind bars.

In *Opposing Viewpoints: Criminal Justice*, several authorities examine the justice and social impact of incarceration in America. In chapters such as Should Sentencing Laws Be Reformed? and What Is the State of the Prison System in the United States? critics and commentators argue the appropriateness of mandatory minimum sentencing laws as well as recidivism rates and rehabilitation programs as part of the ongoing debate over America's incarceration policies. Beyond these concerns, the anthology also includes chapters entitled Are Defendants' Rights Protected in the United States? and Does the Criminal Justice System Need Reform? Together, the authors in *Opposing Viewpoints: Criminal Justice* seek to answer the questions of whether all Americans receive justice at the hands of the police, the courts, and the prison system and whether the justice meted out is making the United States safer and more secure.

 **OPPOSING VIEWPOINTS® SERIES**

 CHAPTER 1

Does the Criminal Justice System Need Reform?

Chapter Preface

In the following chapter, two commentators, Jesselyn Mc-Curdy and Steve Chapman, express their views on the topic of racial profiling by U.S. law enforcement. Although the detaining and harassing of African Americans and Latino Americans has been a controversial subject for some time, and the profiling of Arab Americans has caught the media spotlight since the terrorist attacks on the United States in 2001, racial profiling is only part of a larger concern over racial disparities in the criminal justice system.

With the achievements of the Civil Rights Movement in the 1950s and 1960s, it was widely hoped that all Americans would acquire equal treatment under the law. But for many minority rights' advocates, the promise has not matched reality. In a Citizens' Commission on Civil Rights report from 2000, Ronald Weich and Carlos Angulo wrote:

> Today, our criminal justice system strays far from this ideal. Blacks, Hispanics and other minorities are victimized by disproportionate targeting and unfair treatment by police and other front-line law enforcement officials; by racially skewed charging and plea bargaining decisions of prosecutors; by discriminatory sentencing practices; and by the failure of judges, elected officials, and other criminal justice policymakers to redress the inequities that become more glaring every day.

According to Weich and Angulo, police authorities continue to defend the targeting of blacks and other minorities under the false assumption "that minorities commit the majority of crimes and that therefore it is a sensible use of police resources to focus on the behavior of those individuals." With police operating under this rubric, Weich and Angulo claim that law enforcement and the public naturally expect that more minorities should be arrested, prosecuted, and jailed for their supposed disproportionate share of crimes. For example, in 2000, the state of Pennsylvania noted that minorities composed 66 percent of the state's jail population but only 12 percent of the entire state's population. Across the nation around the same time, analysts found that the Asian American prison population had quadrupled since 1980 and the incarceration rate of Hispanics roughly doubled in the same period. Researchers also claimed that African Americans were 50 percent more likely to receive longer prison sentences than whites and faced the death penalty more often for similar crimes.

Since 2000, several states have begun reform efforts to counteract the trend in racial disparity. Some of these efforts focus on officer training; others emphasize judicial sentencing reform. Most, in the words of the National Criminal Justice Association (NCJA), have met with "limited success." In a 2007 press release, the NCJA contends that greater representation of minorities among police officers, legal counsel, and judges would be a positive step in advancing the notion of equality. But the NCJA also acknowledges that disproportionate incarceration of minorities is still a problem. In 2007, the Governor's Commission on Racial Disparities in Wisconsin recognized that 45 percent of correctional inmates were African Americans while only 6 percent of the state's population was African American. Wisconsin Justice Louis Butler hoped his state's reform efforts would be ongoing until arrest and sentencing practices were back "as they should be." Only continued monitoring of racial disparities will show whether the limited successes will eventually counteract the stubborn national trend.

> *"The grand jury's function as a check on unfounded or intemperate accusations has completely atrophied in a large class of cases."*

Grand Juries Should Be Reformed to Check Prosecutor Power

Stanley S. Arkin

In the following viewpoint, Stanley S. Arkin argues that grand juries have often failed to fulfill their purpose. During grand jury proceedings, a jury of impartial members of a community is supposed to determine if a prosecutor's charges warrant a trial of a named defendant. However, he claims that instead, they give in easily to prosecutors who present spurious claims in an effort to secure indictment. In Arkin's view, prosecutors forego neutrality because they have so much time invested in cases and because their reputations are based on successful indictments. Therefore, Arkin asserts that a magisterial review board should be created to weigh evidence before grand jury proceedings. This additional, impartial group of legal professionals would decide whether a prosecutor has enough legitimate evidence to level a charge in front of a grand jury. Stanley S. Arkin is a defense attorney specializing in business crime. He writes regularly for the New York Law Journal.

As you read, consider the following questions:

1. What document allowed the creation of the grand jury system, according to Arkin?
2. In Arkin's view, why are prosecutors so successful in securing plea bargains from potentially innocent defendants, especially in nonviolent, white-collar criminal cases?
3. Under what federal and state offices does Arkin believe a magisterial review board could be organized?

Our constitutional fathers had prescience but were not omniscient. They well understood that when the decision to indict and the duty to convict are vested in the same person or institution, there is a pronounced risk of abuse and arbitrariness.

Hence the institution of the grand jury, which was included in our Bill of Rights as a "protective bulwark standing solidly between the ordinary citizen and an overzealous prosecutor."

The grand jury has been idealized as an institution in which ordinary citizens determine the propriety of an indictment in a manner designed to sift innocence from guilt and ensure that those undeserving of a criminal charge are shielded from public disclosure of the investigation.

But any realistic observer of our criminal justice system must recognize that, save in highly charged cases such as those involving police shootings or alleged civil rights violations, the indicting grand jury rarely acts as a meaningful check on the prosecutor's charging decisions. The courts have only retrospective oversight of such decisions, and even this is a narrow, constricted procedural review, except conceivably in extreme circumstances. . . .

The Prosecutor Holds the Power of Indictment

As a former New York chief judge once said, grand jurors will "indict a ham sandwich" at the [request] of the prosecutor. The grand jury's function as a check on unfounded or intemperate accusations has completely atrophied in a large class of cases. The authors of a widely cited treatise on grand jury practice have recognized that "the indicting function of the grand jury is no longer of much importance in many jurisdictions."

In practice, the decision whether to indict is in the hands of a prosecutor who, in the words of then-U.S. Attorney General Robert H. Jackson, "has more control over life, liberty and reputation than any other person in America." It is unnerving to note that Mr. Jackson made this observation about prosecutorial power in 1940, before the enactment of the Federal Rules of Criminal Procedure, which gave the prosecutor even greater control over grand jury proceedings; before the proliferation of enormously broad and powerful criminal statutes such as RICO [Racketeer Influenced and Corrupt Organizations Act of 1970]; before many of the interpretations of the federal wire and mail fraud statutes that have criminalized huge swaths of business and government conduct; and before the passage of the Sentencing Guidelines, which tilted the balance of power even further—some might say overwhelmingly—in favor of the federal prosecutor.

Despite the prosecutor's obligations under the law to remain neutral and magisterial, he will always be subject to external pressures that risk distorting his judgment in favor of indictment. Prosecutors are often ambitious and may seek to use their position for personal advancement. Many examples attest to efforts by public prosecutors to move into a broader political role: Rudolph Giuliani turned his highly public prosecutions of white-collar criminals into a mayoralty; Eliot Spitzer, who in his role as New York State Attorney General used his role as prosecutor to extort extraordinary civil tributes to the state, [served as] the state's governor.

The lure of a highly paid partnership in the private criminal defense bar also encourages the prosecutor to distinguish himself in the hope of increasing his worth in the private sector. It is the rare large firm that does not now have at least one partner who can claim to be an "ex-prosecutor"—a pragmatic response to the recent criminalization of much business conduct.

Structural pressures also influence the prosecutor and bias the grand jury's indicting function. Any prosecutor who has devoted months or years to an investigation will have a strong desire to demonstrate that his or her work has not been a waste of time, and will face difficulty—consciously or not—making a truly neutral presentation to the grand jury. This is a particularly dangerous circumstance when, depending upon how a case is presented, the same facts may or may not be viewed as criminal.

A similar instinct gives rise to the recent trend in prosecutions for perjury or obstruction of justice, which are essentially crimes against the prosecutor himself. Although these cases are often justified as necessary to protect the judicial or investigative process, they are also plainly driven by a prosecutor's sense of personal offense at perceived interference with her investigations.

Disrupting Neutrality and Fairness

When we look more broadly at the state of criminal justice in this country—and particularly with respect to economic crimes . . . —the increased potential for abuse in the charging function is a cause for grave concern. The sentences now being handed down for many financial and regulatory crimes are savagely long, both on an absolute basis and when compared to sentences for similar crimes in other countries. [In 2006], in upholding a 25-year sentence for Bernard Ebbers, the former CEO of WorldCom [telecommunications company], the U.S. Court of Appeals for the Second Circuit made the chilling observation that "under the guidelines, it may well be that all but the most trivial frauds in publicly traded companies may trigger sentences amounting to life imprisonment. . . ."

The threat of such sentences gives prosecutors extraordinary leverage in negotiating plea bargains and other concessions from individuals facing indictment. This threat is compounded by the ever-expanding criminalization of a vast amount of non-violent conduct, including the criminalization of the entire federal regulatory system.

The recent forced resignation of eight U.S. attorneys is a stark reminder that prosecutors hold political positions. The sorry spectre of a former senior aide to the attorney general asserting her privilege against self-incrimination when the very matter at issue is whether politics improperly drove the dismissal of these prosecutors raises at the least an uncomfortable negative inference.

Of course, charges that the process has been improperly politicized are nothing new. When Janet Reno announced the summary dismissal of all U.S. attorneys at the beginning of the [Bill] Clinton administration, *The New York Times* lamented that "[a]ny hope that the Clinton administration would operate a Justice Department free of political taint—or even the appearance of political taint—grew dim. . . ." This crucial point—that appearances are important in a legal system that derives its credibility from the presumed neutrality and fairness of the grand jury and prosecutor—applies today with even greater force.

Former U.S. Attorney Mary Jo White . . . dubbed the U.S. District Court for the Southern District of New York the "sovereign district of New York"—an apparent assertion of the independence exhibited by that district. Yet despite the height

The Prosecutor Calls the Shots

Like its more famous relative, the trial jury, the grand jury consists of laypeople who are summoned to the courthouse to fulfill a civic duty. However, the work of the grand jury takes place well before any trial. The primary function of the grand jury is to inquire into the commission of crimes within its jurisdiction and then determine whether an indictment should issue against any particular person. But, in sharp contrast to the trial setting, the jurors hear only one side of the story and there is no judge overseeing the process. With no judge or opposing counsel in the room, grand jurors naturally defer to the prosecutor since he is the most knowledgeable official on the scene. Indeed, the single most important fact to appreciate about the grand jury system is that it is the prosecutor who calls the shots and dominates the entire process. The grand jurors have become little more than window dressing.

W. Thomas Dillard, Stephen R. Johnson, and Timothy Lynch,
Cato Policy Analysis No. 476, May 13, 2003.

ened deference certainly owed to that great institution, it is not insulated from the risk of simply making a wrong call, or calling it wrong for improper purposes. Indeed, U.S. attorneys in the Southern District were recently castigated for placing unconstitutional burdens on the rights of criminal defendants by cutting off their access to legal fees, and also for misrepresenting the facts in the government's defense of that allegation.

Really being untouchable and unreachable are virtues, but insularity, arrogance and unaccountability to neutral review are not.

A Rush to Condemn

In *United States v. Thompson*, the U.S. Court of Appeals for the Seventh Circuit reversed the conviction of a longtime Wisconsin public servant in a prosecution that casts a spotlight on the flaws in our charging process and further undermines the public's perception of our justice system. Georgia Thompson had been charged and convicted under the federal mail fraud statute for depriving Wisconsin of her "honest services." The prosecutor's theory was that Ms. Thompson assisted in steering a public contract to a particular company, the owners of which had previously made lawful campaign contributions to Wisconsin's governor. No evidence was presented that Ms. Thompson "knew or cared about" these lawful contributions, or that the government contract at issue had been awarded for improper political reasons. Ms. Thompson was nonetheless prosecuted on the theory that she had procured a "private gain"—$1,000 annual pay raise that had been approved by Wisconsin's normal civil-service processes, and additional job security. Ms. Thompson was convicted weeks before Wisconsin's 2006 gubernatorial election, and her conviction figured prominently in campaign ads by the incumbent governor's opponents.

In its opinion reversing the conviction, the court observed that:

> Courts can curtail some effects of statutory ambiguity but cannot deal with the source. This prosecution, which led to the conviction and imprisonment of a civil servant for conduct that, as far as this record shows, was designed to pursue the public interest as the employee understood it, may well induce Congress to take another look at the wisdom of enacting ambulatory criminal prohibitions. Haziness designed to avoid loopholes through which bad persons can wriggle can impose high costs on people the statute was not designed to catch.

The prosecution of Ms. Thompson raises serious questions about the risks of prosecutorial discretion in an era of "ambulatory criminal prohibitions," and contributes to growing public cynicism about the fairness and neutrality of our system.

In one of the most highly publicized cases in recent memory, the Duke [University] lacrosse team rape prosecution presents a grievous example of prosecutorial misconduct that is almost unimaginable in a highly developed justice system. Public statements by [Michael] Nifong, the prosecutor, tapped into racial and class biases in Durham [North Carolina] and elsewhere, painting a scenario that so many people seemed to want to believe—one in which a group of privileged young white men, maligned by the prosecutor as "a bunch of hooligans" whose "daddies could buy them expensive lawyers," raped and assaulted a local black woman and then tried to protect one another through a code of silence. As North Carolina's Attorney General Roy Cooper later observed, "there were many points in the case where caution would have served justice better than bravado. And in the rush to condemn, a community and a state lost the ability to see clearly." [The case was dismissed and Nifong disbarred.]

Eroding Trust in the Grand Jury

Events such as these have led to the public perception of a growing "sour spot" in our criminal justice system: The public's trust in the system—the primary basis for its effectiveness and legitimacy—is eroding, it is difficult to be both a hunter and at the same time the warden who determines what may be killed. Yet despite massive increases in the power of the federal prosecutor over the last century, the indicting grand jury has changed little, such that "[a]n attorney familiar with grand jury practice in the early federal courts would notice relatively few changes in the operation of the indicting grand jury." Simply put, this must change if we are to remain the fundamentally decent and humane society envisioned by our forefathers.

Incorporating a Magisterial Review Board

The inherent tension between the prosecutor's magisterial [i.e., impartial] role and the temptation to engage in politics and self-promotion requires new safeguards to protect the integrity of the charging process.

What may be considered is the creation of a dedicated magisterial review board composed of individuals who are trained and sworn to conduct independent reviews of charging decisions by prosecutors. Where a prospective defendant has satisfied a relatively modest showing of reviewability, he or she should have the right to demand that such a review board examine the evidence, evaluate the soundness and fairness of the prosecutor's decision to seek an indictment, and determine whether the charges should be allowed to proceed.

This board would be composed of trained professionals with no stake at all in the outcome of the charging process, whose basic function is to ensure that prosecutorial discretion is exercised legitimately and fairly, and not simply with the goals of winning cases or advancing personal or political agendas. Such a body could be developed within the Department of Justice or our state attorney generals' offices, similar to Inspectors General. While such a review board could not be used to override or replace a grand jury, precharge review by the board would lend particular legitimacy to prosecutions for alleged financial crimes, political corruption, civil rights violations, and other matters that may be expected to generate a significant amount of public agitation and uncertainty.

Significantly, review would not be limited to whether the bare legal minimum of evidence has been amassed to charge a crime, for as Mr. Jackson recognized: "[w]ith the law books filled with a great assortment of crimes, a prosecutor stands a fair chance of finding at least a technical violation of some act on the part of almost anyone." And as the Supreme Court has observed [in *United States v. Lavasco*], there is a strong need for the government to give "full consideration to the desirability of *not prosecuting* in particular cases," in light of the "awesome consequences" that flow from the filing of criminal charges (emphasis supplied).

Socially Productive Judgment

Instead, this body would operate with a higher, magisterial goal, seeking to determine whether the proposed charges reflect a sufficiently humane and socially productive judgment, consistent with the values that gave rise to the grand jury's powers in the first instance.

Such a reviewing body has the benefit of side-stepping most of the routine obstacles to grand jury reform. Many proposals for reform constitute an effort to inject defense lawyers into the grand jury process, or to subject the grand jury to watered-down adversarial aspects of the trial. But such proposals are alien to the traditions and history of the grand jury, which call for flexibility and confidentiality. Moreover, judicial hesitancy to such proposals has focused upon the hard costs and inefficiencies that would flow from making the grand jury process similar to a mini-trial.

A dedicated review process would pose none of these problems. It would impose no additional evidentiary requirements, and would not cabin the prosecutor in presenting his case in any respect. Nor would it require significant judicial supervision. Instead, the board would simply review the results of the investigation, and make an independent assessment of whether charges should be sought. In this way the hunter's role would be separated—not entirely, but meaningfully—from he who determines who should be killed.

There is no question that an additional layer of review such as the proposed magisterial system has potential flaws and risks of abuse. Moreover, we have to acknowledge that the great run of cases are not close ones, at least from the standpoint of determining if mere probable cause exists or charges are justified. And even in these cases there almost always is at least the ceremony of attempting to talk a prosecutor out of a charge—either by seeking a reduction in charges, a deal involving a better charge, or simply through cooperation.

But particularly with regard to non-biblical kinds of crimes, such as those involving the not infrequently muddy corpus delicti of alleged financial impropriety or corruption, our system should seek additional means, such as a form of magisterial review, to better assure less arbitrariness in the all-important charging process.

> *"One way to restore the legitimacy of criminal justice is to return the grand jury to its role as a democratic institution of popular sovereignty."*

Grand Juries Should Be Reformed to Reflect the Communities They Serve

Kevin K. Washburn

In the following viewpoint, Kevin K. Washburn claims that the grand jury system no longer serves the ideals of the nation's founders in representing a check by local communities against unjust laws and prosecutions brought about by central government. Washburn argues that because grand juries are now drawn from jurisdictions that range across a number of communities, they do not reflect localized interests and cannot adequately assess charges pertaining to a specific community. Washburn suggests creating more grand juries—drawn from individual neighborhoods or zip codes—to deal with local crimes that do not have larger implications. He believes that this will restore the original intent of grand juries and increase civic involvement at the local level. Kevin K. Washburn is a professor at the University of Minnesota Law School.

Kevin K. Washburn, "Restoring the Grand Jury," *Fordham Law Review*, vol. 76, April 2008, pp. 2337–2339, 2377–2384. Reproduced by permission.

As you read, consider the following questions:

1. How has the trend toward ensuring diversity on grand juries affected their character, in Washburn's view?

2. Why does Washburn believe that grand juries were probably more effective in early post-colonial America?

3. In what four ways does the author argue that localized grand juries would be more advantageous than grand juries drawn from larger jurisdictions?

Historically, the grand jury was heralded because of its ability to serve as a check by "the people" in the local community on laws imposed by a central government that was more distant from ordinary citizens. The grand jury was intended by the Anti-Federalists [at the time of Independence, the Anti-Federalists argued for stronger states' rights] to be a check on federal authority. As the Supreme Court has looked increasingly toward originalist interpretations of the Constitution to determine constitutional meaning in cases involving criminal procedure, the Court could use such an interpretive lens to restore life to the Fifth Amendment's grand jury requirement. Today, grand juries rarely serve the purposes envisioned by the founders.

One need not be an originalist, however, to want to restore power to the grand jury. A legal realist who is skeptical of the power of the rule of law and the outcome of court decisions may also see benefits in restoring decision making to community groups that have a different agenda than judges. . . .

No Longer Serving Communities

Though minority communities and the founding era's Anti-Federalists may seem like strange bedfellows in the post-civil rights era, they actually may have something in common: a mistrust of federal (prosecutorial) power and a belief that such power can be an instrument of abuse of local citizens.

Ironically, the grand jury may have lost its ability to serve in its constitutionally envisioned role as community representative and protector of local communities precisely because of the manner in which federal courts have sought to insure diversity on juries. Under the current regime, diversity in the grand jury is sought by assembling a grand jury from a pool that represents "a fair cross-section of the community" within the entire jurisdiction. While this general principle may reflect good intentions, courts have interpreted it to presume that any given jurisdiction comprises a single "community." In reality, each jurisdiction comprises numerous communities that can be defined along many different lines.

In adopting the artificial notion that each jurisdiction is a single community and then attempting to assemble jury pools that mirror the diversity of the entire jurisdiction, courts dilute the representation of each of the communities and suffocate the grand jury's ability to represent any distinct community well. As a result, the jury pool, and ultimately the grand jury, may constitute a fair cross-section of a jurisdiction, but most certainly does not represent a fair cross-section of any one community. Put differently, courts have interpreted the "cross-sectional ideal" in a manner that suffocates the "community ideal."

The unfortunate practical effects of such a regime are myriad. The districtwide grand jury that has the responsibility to review narcotics cases from the urban inner city or the violent crime case from the distant Native American reservation may have no residents from either of those communities serving as a juror. Yet, in a society that remains highly segregated, it may be far more important that each community is represented accurately and fairly in important local institutions of criminal justice, than that each community have token membership in a jurisdictionwide institution. . . .

Changing the Grand Jury's Structure, Not Its Purpose

The way to restore the "independence" of the grand jury, and really the essential purpose of the grand jury, is to recognize the grand jury's political and representative nature and to restore the attributes that would allow it to maintain relevance. The insight offered by Professors Albert Alschuler and Andrew Deiss [law scholars who are experts on the history of juries] that the grand jury's "role in American civic life declined" as its "composition became more democratic" ought to be viewed as a profound tragedy. The grand jury has an important role to play in a governmental system that necessarily sacrifices local legitimacy when it locates power in various central (and distant) governmental authorities. One way to restore the legitimacy of criminal justice is to return the grand jury to its role as a democratic institution of popular sovereignty.

To restore this role, we need not change the way the grand jury works; we merely need to change the way that it is constructed. If the grand jury is properly viewed as a quasi-political institution—an institution that emerged not so much as a substantive, but as a political check on the legislature and the prosecutor—it should be constructed in a manner that allows it to meet its quasi-political purpose. And given this quasi-political role, a grand jury must be constructed differently than a trial jury.

Forming Neighborhood Grand Juries

To make the grand jury more effective as a political institution, it is necessary to minimize the gap between the grand jury and the community it represents. Put another way, we need to solve the agency problem to align the interests of the grand jury more closely with the interests of the community it serves.

Though "propertied white males" was an artificial community [in early America when grand juries came into being as part of the Bill of Rights] that looks too narrow in hindsight, the grand jury presumably represented that constituency well. On the community's behalf, the grand jury refused to apply laws enacted by a central government that were unpopular locally. While no one would argue for a return to grand juries composed only of propertied white males, one who yearns for the return of the "independent" grand jury may well wish for a grand jury that better represents each community and that is more tightly constructed. By giving community members a much more meaningful role in criminal justice, such a grand jury could help to restore the legitimacy of criminal justice in each community.

In an increasingly diverse society, opportunities for citizen participation ought to be enhanced, not minimized. With this in mind, one potential solution is to increase the number of grand juries and to "localize" them. In other words, the solution to the grand jury problem may not be to provide different tools to the grand jury, or even to insure through affirmative action that each grand jury has some number of minority members. The solution may not be instrumental. Rather the solution is political. The grand jury should be gerrymandered—not racially, but geographically.

Instead of a districtwide or countywide grand jury, each jurisdiction should construct numerous "neighborhood grand juries" that represent much smaller constituencies and that are thus likely to be more closely aligned with the communities (or neighborhoods) that they represent. Consider perhaps a "grand jury by zip code" approach. A grand jury in each zip code would vastly expand the involvement of the local community in criminal justice. Another way to achieve the same ideal, using existing political boundaries, would be to choose small political districts, such as House [of Representatives] legislative districts or city council districts. Professor Adriaan Lanni has put forth a similar proposal in a much wider context, arguing that "grand and petit juries" should be "drawn from a small catchment area representing the local community."

As Professor Lanni has suggested, it is not at all clear what would be the most efficacious means of selecting the definition of "community" for such purposes. However, the notion here is that a grand jury that is more localized could replicate the kind of community that existed when the Bill of Rights came into being and could meet the constitutionally intended purposes of the Grand Jury Clause more closely. Consider that the population of Boston around the time of the adoption of the Bill of Rights numbered approximately 18,000 residents, a substantial percentage of whom were women and children and others who could not serve on a grand jury.

In a society that is far more heavily populated and much more diverse, we ask too much from a grand jury that is culled from an entire county or judicial district. The representation of each community in such a grand jury is diluted to the point that the grand jury is effectively homogenized. Such a grand jury simply cannot serve the same role as these earlier grand juries, which represented a modest-sized community of similarly situated people.

Consider a large, diverse city like Los Angeles. Perhaps there should be 150 or more grand juries scattered at various places across the city. Such a decentralized model would give greater voice to subcommunities in Los Angeles and insure that the diversity that exists on the streets is actually represented in this governmental institution.

Crime Is Often a Community Problem and Should Involve Community Response

The most compelling cases for the use of localized grand juries arise for those offenses that have a distinctly local impact, for example, cases where both the victim and the defendant are members of the same community. Most crimes against

Expanding the Power of Local Grand Juries to Promote Community Justice

The basic principle of community justice—local, popular participation in all aspects of the administration of justice—can be readily advanced by existing institutions: the grand jury and the petit jury. Grand and petit jurors drawn from the local community would be far more representative than the volunteers in community justice programs. A series of reforms would transform the grand jury procedure from a passive rubber stamp of the prosecutor's charges to an interactive process that permits the jury to suggest alternative charges. Grand juries convened as focus groups would also provide more generalized input into charging policies. Perhaps most importantly, the jury would be permitted to decide the sanction through procedures that encourage, but do not mandate, restorative and rehabilitative sentencing outcomes. This approach would alleviate some of the distortions in the current process of generating sentencing laws and law enforcement policies, and would permit local communities, particularly those that suffer from high crime rates, to strike their own balance between security and the social costs of stringent sentencing laws.

Adriaan Lanni,
Harvard Civil Rights-Civil Liberties Law Review,
Summer 2005.

persons and many narcotics offenses meet these criteria. Hearing such cases in the neighborhood grand jury can increase the notion of self-determination at the local level. When an offense occurs at the local level and primarily affects people within a single community, it is more difficult to justify interference from a broad central authority. On the other hand, crimes that involve outsiders present different problems. There, the costs of using local grand juries may exceed the benefits.

While some may doubt the salience of the localized geographic community in an increasingly atomized physical world in which many people are far more connected to nongeographic communities defined by professional connections or other communities developed through Internet capabilities, geographic communities are still highly salient to many of the most common crimes. Violent crime, for example, affects one's sense of physical safety and has the most significant effects on people within the zone of risk of such events.

The Advantages of Neighborhood Grand Juries for Local Offenses

The neighborhood grand jury or "grand jury by zip code" approach offers numerous benefits consistent with all of the original virtues of the grand jury. Consider the advantages of jury service cited by the Supreme Court and commentators and how much more effectively they would be served by such an approach. . . .

A grand jury in each community would insure that far more citizens would be able to serve in a meaningful role in criminal justice. The educative value to the citizenry of the increased volume of citizen participation would be tremendous, but the substance of the education would be improved as well. Because members of the grand jury would be educated about crime in their own community, grand jury service might help motivate greater action in addressing crime. As the world we inhabit has become much more atomized, grand jury service would help to reconnect members of a community around a specific problem that is highly important to that community. . . .

A grand jury constructed from a single zip code or neighborhood would also be much more effective in providing the "voice" of the community. . . . Of course, the voice of the community may now have an accent or use a different language entirely, as the number of languages spoken in the United States has increased dramatically. To give the grand jury its intended purpose, however, each of those voices must be heard.

Any jurisdiction has multiple community voices. Legitimacy will be fully restored only when the criminal justice system can hear each of the substantial voices present in the jurisdiction. Substantial criminal justice scholarship suggests that legitimacy is better served when the community is invested in fair criminal justice processes. In turn, the rule of law is served. Citizens are more likely to comply with the law and cooperate with police in investigations. . . .

A Better Check on Prosecutor Power

The neighborhood grand jury model would inevitably have some ramifications for prosecutorial power. As it stands, the grand jury often covers such broad jurisdiction that it does not likely feel invested in—or knowledgeable about—the community where the crime occurred. Each grand juror is likely to have different interests and none is likely to necessarily have a very strong interest in any given case. Indeed, some may feel simply inconvenienced by being required to serve and bored by the substance of the testimony. These circumstances may heighten the power of the prosecutor and law enforcement officials in several ways. Such grand juries are less likely to exercise their own curiosity about investigations, are more likely to accede to the prosecutorial momentum, and are perhaps more likely to defer to these law enforcement experts who know more than any single grand juror about the community in which the crime occurred.

On the other hand, a grand jury drawn entirely from one community is more likely to know as much, collectively at least, about the neighborhood as the prosecutor and law enforcement agents. Moreover, such a grand jury is likely to be even more interested in crime and criminal justice policy in that neighborhood. Finally, it is also more likely to unite around these important concerns. Unless the prosecutor resides in the same neighborhood as the grand jurors, she may be viewed with skepticism. As a result, the prosecutor may be less successful in making the grand jury her "handmaiden," to borrow a term from Professor [Niki] Kuckes. Indeed, one clear way to change the balance of power between the grand jury and the prosecutor is to tighten up the bonds between the grand jurors so that the grand jury is emboldened and self-confident.

To many scholars, the most damning criticisms of criminal justice have centered on problems of race. To address such problems, many scholars have focused on solutions designed to achieve racially balanced or racially representative juries. The solution sketched out here avoids controversial strategies such as affirmative action based on race, yet yields some of the same benefits that those strategies might provide. As others have demonstrated, not all racial problems require race-based solutions. In an era of a "color-blind" Constitution, this approach may be attractive.

Potential Disadvantages of Neighborhood Grand Juries

The neighborhood grand jury poses some risks that may be troubling in some contexts. To the extent that the purpose here is to free the community, as represented by the grand jury, to prefer its own normative policy judgments over those of a central legislature, one could imagine certain circumstances in which the grand jury will behave in a manner inconsistent with rule-of-law values. For example, a grand jury may be less protective of a suspect who is from outside the local community, and therefore it might be more inclined to issue an unwarranted indictment. This might be called the "false positive" effect. Or, on the other hand, a grand jury may be too protective of the member of the community, and thereby decline to issue a righteous indictment. This might be called a "false negative."

These are serious potential problems, and the best way to address them is perhaps to retain jurisdictionwide grand juries for some offenses and to use community grand juries primarily for local offenses with local suspects and local victims. For localized offenses, like most violent offenses, the relative interest in the offense in the local community is high and the relative interest by the central authority is low. Thus, the central government has a much lesser claim to legitimate concern. On the other hand, for offenses with national or regional impacts, or that cross jurisdictional boundaries, the central authority has greater legitimacy, and a grand jury with a wider reach may be more appropriate.

> "Current law enforcement guidelines do little to stop officials from relying on race or ethnicity when deciding to initiate traffic stops or other investigative activities."

Law Enforcement Should Cease Racial Profiling

Jesselyn McCurdy

In the following viewpoint, Jesselyn McCurdy argues that law enforcement has used racial profiling to harass and detain millions of innocent Americans because of their ethnicity or skin color. McCurdy claims that blacks, Latinos, Arab Americans, and other minorities are no more likely to commit crimes than white Americans and therefore should not be singled out by law enforcement as probable drug dealers, gang members, or terrorists. In McCurdy's opinion, racial profiling simply increases tension and fear while wasting police resources needed to track down real criminals. Jesselyn McCurdy is a legislative counsel at the American Civil Liberties Union's office in Washington, D.C.

As you read, consider the following questions:

1. What "constitutional commitment" does racial profiling violate, in McCurdy's view?

Jesselyn McCurdy, "Racial Profiling: 'Wrong in America'," *Afro-Netizen*, December 7, 2007. Reproduced by permission of the publisher and the author.

2. What groups does McCurdy claim have been especially targeted for racial profiling since September 11, 2001?

3. As the author relates, what two members of Congress are co-sponsoring the End Racial Profiling Act of 2007?

[In 1955], Rosa Parks' quiet but determined resistance sparked the Montgomery [Alabama] bus boycott and a movement that would eventually end legal segregation by race in America. While the racial myths and stereotypes formerly used to justify segregation may be less obvious today, they are still a potent force in American life, and those stereotypes are perhaps nowhere more persistent and harmful than within the criminal justice system.

Racial profiling by law enforcement agents is based on racial stereotypes. Random traffic stops and arrests and deciding who to target for criminal investigations relying on skin color and ethnicity rather than probable cause is not only morally culpable and un-American, the end result is ineffective law enforcement. This practice violates our nation's core values and our basic constitutional commitment to equal justice under the law.

Persecuting People of Color

Repeated studies have shown that African Americans, Latinos and other people of color are no more likely, and very often less likely, to be involved in illegal activity than whites. Americans began to understand the concept of racial profiling in the late '80s and early '90s as advocacy groups and the media began to uncover ways in which people of color are harassed on a regular basis by police for no reason. Millions of innocent motorists on highways across the country are victims of racial profiling. The "war on drugs" and more recently "the war on terror" have given law enforcement an excuse to target people who fit their image of a "drug courier," "gang member," or "terrorist."

Prior to 9/11, African Americans, Native Americans and Latinos were often the targets of police profiling. And since the terrorist attacks of September 11, 2001, law enforcement has intensified the profiling and harassment of South Asians, Muslims and Arabs based on their national origin, ethnicity and religion.

Racial profiling is the first step down the long road of a criminal justice system that results in the heavily disproportionate incarceration of people of color, especially young men, for drug-related crimes, and of Arabs, Muslims and South Asians for suspicion of terrorism. People of color are no more likely than whites to use or sell drugs, and Arabs, Muslims and South Asians are no more likely than whites to be terrorists.

Wasting Resources and Generating Fear

President [George W.] Bush vowed to end racial profiling, calling it "wrong in America." But current law enforcement guidelines do little to stop officials from relying on race or ethnicity when deciding to initiate traffic stops or other investigative activities. Policies primarily designed to impact certain groups, however, are ineffective and often result in the destruction of civil liberties for everyone.

Singling out African Americans, Latinos, Muslims, Arabs and South Asians for special law enforcement scrutiny without a reasonable belief that they are involved in a crime results in little evidence of actual criminal activity and wastes important police resources. Racial profiling makes us all less safe by diverting limited law enforcement resources and by targeting innocent individuals for government scrutiny. Law enforcement agents conflate race and ethnicity with criminal intent and activity. While African Americans, Latinos and other people of color, are the first victims of racial profiling, ultimately everyone is victimized when justice is color conscious.

The Many Names of Racial Profiling

The criminalization of race takes on special meaning in the context of traffic stops. Statistics and studies overwhelmingly support the contention that racial profiling—commonly described as "the detention, interdiction or other disparate treatment of an individual [by police] solely on the basis of the racial or ethnic status of such individual"—has occurred for decades on our nation's streets and highways. This has led commentators to assert that dark skin, by itself, effectively functions as probable cause to stop a vehicle and conduct a search. The notion that many officers pursue race-conscious policing policies has even made it into the popular lexicon in the form of the terms "driving while black" or "driving while brown"—which some facetiously describe as "unwritten violation[s] in the state's traffic code." This phenomenon has been referenced in newspapers, academic journals, and even popular culture. For instance, an animated cartoon series on cable television recently depicted a scene in which a police officer stopped an African American and asked, "Do you know how 'black' you were going?" The puzzled motorist responded, "Somewhere between Denzel Washington and Nelly?"

Anthony E. Mucchetti, Harvard Latino Law Review, *2005.*

[In December of 2007] House Judiciary Chairman John Conyers (D-MI) and Senator Russ Feingold (D-WI) [introduced] the End Racial Profiling Act . . . (ERPA), which will prohibit federal law enforcement agencies from engaging in racial profiling and encourage states to adopt the same type of ban on the practice. The legislation will also permit victims of racial profiling to take legal action and requires states to establish procedures for victims to file complaints against police officers who racially profile. In addition, the bill provides data collection demonstration and best practice incentive grants to state and local law enforcement agencies

Congressional leaders should support Conyers and Feingold in bringing this legislation to the floor and ensuring maximum support for the bills. The Democratic leadership should be eager to move on this legislation in a year when every Democratic presidential candidate has condemned racial profiling and when even unusual suspects such as the International Association of Police Chiefs and President Bush recognize that racial profiling is both wrong and harmful. Ending legal segregation took 68 years to accomplish, from the 1896 *Plessy* [*v. Ferguson*] decision to the 1964 Civil Rights Act, and one of the most massive human rights movements the world has witnessed. Ending racial profiling shouldn't take that long.

"[Surveys show] law enforcement to be admirably colorblind when it comes to routine traffic enforcement."

Law Enforcement Does Not Engage in Racial Profiling

Steve Chapman

In the following viewpoint, Steve Chapman contends that police officers do not engage in racial profiling. Using statistics that show that minority motorists are stopped at nearly the same rate as white motorists, Chapman asserts that fears of unjust, racist treatment of minorities are unfounded. Chapman acknowledges that African American motorists, for example, may be arrested at higher rates during traffic stops, but he attributes this finding to the fact that blacks are statistically more likely to engage in crime and have outstanding warrants than white motorists. Steve Chapman is a columnist for the Chicago Tribune.

As you read, consider the following questions:

1. Which government agency conducted the survey of law enforcement on which Chapman bases his argument?

2. What group labeled the government survey findings "disturbing," as Chapman relates?

Steve Chapman, "The Racial Profiling Myth Lives On," *Chicago Tribune*, May 6, 2007. Reproduced by permission.

3. Why does Chapman state that the "cops can't win" in the racial profiling debate?

We've all heard of the offense of "driving while black." But not everyone has heard the good news: It doesn't exist anymore. According to an authoritative report, black motorists are no more likely than whites to be pulled over by police. So how has that study been greeted? As proof that police racism is still a powerful force.

It's a widely accepted article of faith that cops systematically engage in racial profiling against dark-complexioned folks. Yet this is the second consecutive survey from the federal Bureau of Justice Statistics [BJS]—using information supplied not by police but by citizens—that finds law enforcement to be admirably colorblind when it comes to routine traffic enforcement. Not a puny achievement, but one that was overlooked by people straining to find lingering discrimination.

No Evidence of Racism

The complaint is that though they get stopped at the same rate as whites, minority motorists are more likely to get unfavorable treatment during the stop. According to BJS, 3.6 percent of whites are searched, compared with 9.5 percent of blacks and 8.8 percent of Latinos. African-Americans are more likely to have force used against them and to be arrested. And they more often feel their treatment is unwarranted.

What can we make of these figures? Not what is claimed by critics like those at the American Civil Liberties Union, which labeled the disparities "disturbing," and columnist Eugene Robinson of *The Washington Post*, who detected "powerful evidence that racial profiling is alive and well." Some people get their exercise jumping to conclusions.

The researchers at BJS tried to discourage snap judgments. "The apparent disparities documented in this report do not

Race/Hispanic Origin of All Drivers Compared to Drivers Stopped by Police in 2002					
Demographic Characteristic	U.S. Population age 16 or older	Population Who Drive a Few Times a Year or More		Drivers Stopped by Police in 2002	
		Number	Percent	Number	Percent
Total	215,536,780	192,687,190	89.4%	16,783,467	8.7%
White	157,373,713	146,779,643	93.3%	12,842,254	8.7%
Black	25,694,070	20,260,621	78.9	1,852,086	9.1
Hispanic	23,955,183	18,619,405	77.7	1,595,872	8.6
Other race	8,513,815	7,000,729	82.2	493,256	7.0

Note: Detail may not add to total because of rounding.

TAKEN FROM: Mathew R. Durose, Erica L. Schmitt, and Patrick A. Langan, Contacts between Police and the Public: Finding from the 2002 National Survey, April 2005.

constitute proof that police treat people differently along demographic lines," they warn. "Any of these disparities might be explained by countless other factors and circumstances that were not taken into account in the analysis."

Odds That Favor Arrest

Plenty of other elements could generate these divergent patterns. Why would black drivers be arrested more often? Maybe because African-Americans commit crimes at a far higher rate and are convicted of felonies at a far higher rate. In 2005, for instance, blacks were nearly seven times more likely to be in prison than whites.

Those disparities are bound to affect the outcome of traffic stops. Most blacks, like most whites, are not crooks. But since the average black driver is statistically more likely to be a criminal than the average white driver, he's more likely to have an outstanding arrest warrant—which the police would find when running a computer check of his license. A computer check that turns up a long rap sheet will probably induce the patrol officer to ask for a look inside the trunk.

A motorist of felonious habits is also more likely to have illegal guns or drugs on board. If the contraband is visible to a traffic cop, or if it shows up in a search, the driver can expect to be arrested. Not to mention that the vehicle itself may turn out to be stolen.

Given the racial gap in crime rates, it would be a shock if traffic stops didn't generate more searches and arrests of blacks than whites. Even in a world where cops are completely free of racial prejudice, that is exactly what you would expect. There is a similar difference, after all, between the sexes—males are nearly twice as likely as females to be arrested during a stop. Is that because cops are sexists? No, it's because men commit more crimes.

The Cops Cannot Win

Trying to find "compelling" evidence of racism in this data is a fruitless task. Robinson makes much of the fact that blacks who are stopped are more likely to be sent on their way without any corrective action, even an oral warning. That, he says, "suggests there was no good reason to stop these people." Or it might suggest that cops cut African-American motorists a bit more slack on petty issues, perhaps in the hope of improving their reputation.

Whatever they do, the cops can't win. Blacks don't get stopped more often? Big deal. Blacks have higher arrest rates? Proof of racism. More blacks are let off without a warning? More proof of racism.

And if fewer blacks were let off without a warning? I'll let you guess how that would be interpreted.

"Open civilian trials in federal court best respect the rule of law, fundamental American values, and constitutional rights."

Terrorism Suspects Should Be Tried in Federal Court

Carl Tobias

In the following viewpoint, Carl Tobias argues that terrorism suspects should—in most cases—be tried for their crimes in federal courts. Tobias states that conducting terrorism trials in the courts demonstrates to the world America's commitment to the rule of law. He asserts that to try all terrorism suspects by military tribunal—as the George W. Bush administration favors—would impose an undue level of secrecy and likely rob suspects of rights that are afforded in the civilian court system. Carl Tobias is a professor at the University of Richmond School of Law.

As you read, consider the following questions:

1. What U.S. Supreme Court case does Tobias invoke in asserting that military tribunals would not guarantee defendants' rights?

Carl Tobias, "Why Terrorism Suspects Should Be Tried in Federal Court, Not Before Military Tribunals: Lessons from the Moussaoui Mess," *FindLaw*, August 29, 2006. Reproduced by permission.

2. For what reasons does Tobias claim that the trial of Zacarias Moussaoui may be a worst-case scenario in exemplifying how justice in terrorism cases can be obtained in civilian courts?

3. According to the author, when might trial by military tribunal be acceptable for terrorism suspects?

[In spring 2006], a federal jury in Alexandria, Virginia concluded that the death penalty should not be imposed on Zacarias Moussaoui, the admitted Al Qaeda member whom the United States charged with failing to speak to interrogators about the 9/11 plot.

Moussaoui's tortured prosecution consumed years, and, in the end, the government did not convince the jury to impose the punishment it sought. Now that some time has passed, it is possible to derive several lessons from Moussaoui's capital punishment proceeding.

Terrorism Suspects Can, and Sometimes Should, Be Tried in Regular Federal Courts

First and foremost, Moussaoui's prosecution illustrates the necessity of trying suspected terrorists in our regular, civilian federal courts—as opposed to military tribunals or other similar options. These proceedings are open and public, and in them, most constitutional rights must be honored.

Such trials serve a number of important public values. First, they enable the people of the United States, and the international community, to see that America honors the rule of law not only when its own citizens are on trial, but for all.

During the Moussaoui trial, for example, at several critical junctures, U.S. District Judge Leonie Brinkema exhibited considerable solicitude for Moussaoui's rights—such as his Sixth Amendment right to confront witnesses against him. In particular, at one juncture, Judge Brinkema directed the government to give Moussaoui access to three Al Qaeda prisoners

---

Treat Terrorists as Criminals, Not Freedom Fighters

Those who commit terrorist acts should be tried as the criminals they are, instead of the "warriors" they claim to be. If the Guantánamo detainees were prosecuted in federal courts instead of being designated as "combatants," most by now would be serving prison time as convicted terrorists, instead of being celebrated as victims or freedom fighters.

Kelly Anne Moore, New York Times, *August 21, 2007.*

---

detained overseas, among them two major players, Ramzi Binalshibh and Khalid Shaikh Mohammed. Moussaoui claimed Binalshibh and Mohammed's testimony could exculpate him. However, the government did not ultimately provide these witnesses—citing national security concerns. Moreover, the Fourth Circuit reversed Judge Brinkema on this issue.

The right to confront witnesses is just one of the rights to which defendants are constitutionally entitled. Defendants also have a right to an attorney, the right to a jury drawn from the community, and a right to an open courtroom except in extraordinary circumstances. As the Supreme Court recognized recently in *Hamdan v. Rumsfeld*, the military tribunals envisioned by the [George W.] Bush Administration, which it created through an Executive Order, would not have accorded defendants such rights.

Moussaoui's Trial May Well Be a Worst-Case Scenario

Obviously, the Moussaoui trial itself was not ideal. But it's important to remember that Moussaoui's criminal trial might well present the worst-case scenario—for several reasons.

Moussaoui insisted on representing himself—though Judge Brinkema wisely allowed stand-by counsel to remain in the courtroom as a backstop—and his conduct was erratic. His lawyers argued, very plausibly, that he was mentally ill. His own testimony damned him—indeed, it seemed toward the end of trial, to have enabled the government to grasp victory from the jaws of defeat. And finally, after the jury rendered its decision, Moussaoui attempted to withdraw his year-old guilty plea, a request the judge promptly rejected.

But Moussaoui's was far from a typical case—and this bizarre proceeding is no reason to deny other terrorism suspects public trials in civilian courts.

Significantly, several other prosecutions of suspected terrorists have proceeded much more smoothly. Illustrative have been the trials of three men—Ali al-Timimi, Ahmed Omar Abu Ali and Ali Asad Chandia—who allegedly were members of the so-called "Virginia jihad network." Federal prosecutors rather easily secured convictions of the three defendants in the U.S. District Court for the Eastern District of Virginia, the court on which Judge Brinkema sits.

And imagine how poorly—and summarily—a proceeding like Moussaoui's might have gone before a military tribunal, especially one like that contemplated in the Executive Order, which the Supreme Court rejected. Such a tribunal might have been inclined to accept Moussaoui's admissions of guilt without querying if they had arisen from mental illness, and might have been sorely tempted to recommend execution even of a very likely mentally-ill man.

Even if the Moussaoui trial wasn't, in the end, a model of justice, Judge Brinkema was, in many respects, a model judge. Would a military tribunal be as fair, impartial, and concerned with honoring constitutional rights as Judge Brinkema showed herself to be? Not likely.

Do Not Let the Exception Destroy the Rule

Ideally, the U.S. ought to make case-by-case decisions about the appropriate tribunal in which to prosecute suspected terrorists—and in most cases, ought to opt for open trials in federal civilian court.

Granted, a few trials may be so sensitive, from a national security perspective, that using a tribunal might be justified. But such trials will be rare. There are numerous available mechanisms, short of using a secret tribunal and ignoring constitutional rights, that will protect security. Only in situations that would clearly jeopardize national security by revealing highly delicate material in open court, should the U.S. consider optional fora, such as military tribunals.

In the end, open civilian trials in federal court best respect the rule of law, fundamental American values, and constitutional rights. If we opt not to use them, that decision should be rare.

Periodical Bibliography

The following articles have been selected to supplement the diverse views presented in this chapter.

Rod Blagojevich et al.	"Better Models for Juvenile Justice," *Christian Science Monitor*, August 22, 2007.
Brian R. Farrell	"The Rights of Detainees," *America*, September 24, 2007.
John Gibeaut	"Indictment of a System," *ABA Journal*, January 2001.
Sarah Hammond	"Adults or Kids?" *State Legislatures*, April 2008.
Dahlia Lithwick	"Getting Away with Torture," *Newsweek*, May 5, 2008.
John Reitzel and Alex R. Piquero	"Does It Exist? Studying Citizens' Attitudes of Racial Profiling," *Police Quarterly*, June 2006.
Wesley G. Skogan	"Why Reforms Fail," *Policing & Society*, March 2008.
Jerome H. Skolnick	"Racial Profiling—Then and Now," *Criminology & Public Policy*, February 2007.
Lois Spear	"Reforming the System," *America*, July 31, 2006.
Robert Spencer	"Why Profiling Is Necessary," *Human Events*, August 21, 2006.
Stuart Taylor Jr.	"Innocents in Prison," *National Journal*, August 4, 2007.
Amy Waldman	"Prophetic Justice," *Atlantic Monthly*, October 2006.

OPPOSING
VIEWPOINTS®
SERIES

CHAPTER 2

What Is the State of the Prison System in the United States?

Chapter Preface

In February 2008, the Pew Center on the States' Public Safety Performance Project reported that 2,319,258 Americans were incarcerated in U.S. jails and prisons, making the ratio of imprisoned adults about one in 100. The cost of retaining this number of individuals in prison has also grown with the prison population. The Pew report states that in 2007, state corrections spending reached $49 billion, an increase of $11 billion over 1987 corrections spending. However, according to the Pew Center, the impact of this high incarceration rate and increase in spending has not obviously reduced crime. Adam Gelb, director of the Public Safety Performance Project, states, "For all the money spent on corrections today, there hasn't been a clear and convincing return for public safety."

One way federal, state, and local governments are attempting to mitigate the cost of corrections is through the use of private prisons. With the prison population continuing to grow, and current jail and prison facilities unable to meet these increasing needs, some states have begun to turn to private companies to house the swelling number of inmates. One state that has already invested in the privatization program is Texas. Marc A. Levin, director of the Center for Effective Justice at the Texas Public Policy Foundation, is quoted in *BusinessWeek* in 2006 touting the benefits of private prisons. He claims, "Savings in Texas from private prisons have been estimated at 10% to 14%. Moreover, private facilities, such as those run by Corrections Corp. of America, often provide far better access to programs such as drug treatment and job training. Such programs have also been demonstrated to reduce recidivism."

Even with the apparent benefits—both in economic terms and in terms of public safety—many still argue that the cons of private prisons require careful consideration before widespread privatization is adopted. Josh Jackson highlights many of the negative aspects of private prisons in a 2006 article in *Next American City*. He writes, "Private prisons generally reduce salaries, healthcare, and training [of prison staff]," and he mentions one instance in which poor staff training resulted in the escape of four murderers and two additional violent offenders from a private Youngstown, Ohio, prison. Jackson also argues that private prisons do not have the best interests of prisoners or the public in mind when they offer their services. He quotes independent prison analyst Judith A. Greene who points out that private companies are by definition out to do what is best for business, not what's necessarily best for the public. She goes on to argue that as a result, many of the decisions made to increase profit, such as "skimping on food, medical services, and prison programs," jeopardize the institution's ability to ready prisoners for a return to society.

While the impact of private prisons on the criminal justice system remains to be seen, the rate of inmate incarceration in American prisons—both public and private—continues to rise. Debate over how to best run these prisons will undoubtedly continue as long as there are crimes being committed and inmates being detained. The authors in the following chapter address the state of the prison system in the United States and debate the pros and cons of different programs being used within prison walls.

*"We should not suppose that . . . we im-
prison too many people."*

High Incarceration Rates
Decrease Crime Rates

James Q. Wilson

*In the following viewpoint, James Q. Wilson argues that high in-
carceration rates in the United States are responsible for the national crime rate reduction. He contends that prison sentences
both deter individuals from committing criminal acts and also
prevent crimes by incapacitating criminals. While acknowledging
the shortcomings of the prison system, the author maintains that
when compared to other Western countries, the U.S. rates of imprisonment still benefit the population as a whole. Wilson's academic career in public policy began in 1961. He currently teaches
at Pepperdine University in California, and he has authored numerous books on crime, morality, and government. Additionally,
he has served on numerous public policy commissions within the
federal government since 1966.*

As you read, consider the following questions:

1. By what percent has the crime rate decreased due to the
   increased prison population? According to whom?

James Q. Wilson, "Do the Time, Lower the Crime," *Los Angeles Times*, March 30,
2008. www.latimes.com. Reproduced by permission of the author.

2. Based on the information given by the author, how do the robbery and imprisonment rates in the United States compare with other Western countries?

3. According to Wilson, how many felons are on probation and why?

Do we have too many people in prison?

If you read a [2008] report by the Pew Center on the States [a research institute that formulates public policy], you would think so. As its title proclaimed, more than one in 100 American adults is in jail or prison. For young black males, the number is one in nine.

The report's authors contend that the incarceration rate represents a problem because the number of felons serving time does not have a "clear impact" on crime rates—and that all those inmates are costing taxpayers too much money to house. But nowhere in the report is there any discussion of the effect of prison on crime, and the argument about costs seems based on the false assumption that we are locking people up at high rates for the wrong reasons.

The Overwhelming Benefits of Prisons

In the last 10 years, the effect of prison on crime rates has been studied by many scholars. The Pew report doesn't mention any of them. Among them is [economist] Steven Levitt, coauthor of "Freakonomics." He and others have shown that states that sent a higher fraction of convicts to prison had lower rates of crime, even after controlling for all of the other ways (poverty, urbanization and the proportion of young men in the population) that the states differed. A high risk of punishment reduces crime. Deterrence works.

But so does putting people in prison. The typical criminal commits from 12 to 16 crimes a year (not counting drug offenses). Locking him up spares society those crimes. Several scholars have separately estimated that the increase in the size of our prison population has driven down crime rates by 25%.

The Pew writers lament the fact that this country imprisons a higher fraction of its population than any other nation in the world, including Russia. But what they ignore is what the United States gets in return for its high rate of incarceration. For instance, in 1976, Britain had a lower robbery rate than did California. But then California got tough on crime as judges began handing out more prison sentences, and Britain became soft as laws were passed encouraging judges to avoid prison sentences. As a result, the size of the state's prison population went up while Britain's went down. By 1996, Britain's robbery rate was one-quarter higher than California's. Compared with those of the U.S. overall, Britain's burglary and assault rates are twice as high, according to a comparative study done by the U.S. Bureau of Justice Statistics.

These differences in crime rates involve many countries with low imprisonment rates. The robbery rate in the U.S. is not only lower than that in Britain but also that in Australia, Canada, the Netherlands, Poland, Portugal, Scotland and Spain, according to the same study. The imprisonment rate in these countries is one-fifth to one-tenth that in the United States.

You cannot make an argument about the cost of prisons without taking into account the benefit of prisons. The Pew report makes no effort to do this. Instead, it argues that spending on prisons may be crowding out spending on education. For instance, tax dollars spent on higher education in the U.S. have increased much more slowly than those spent on corrections. The report does not ask whether the slower growth may be in part because of the sharp increase in private support for public universities, much less whether society gets as much from universities as it does from prisons.

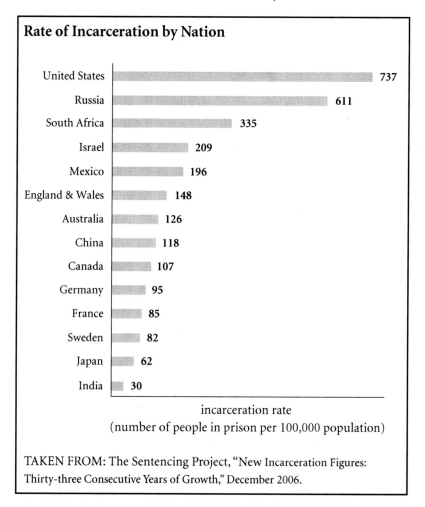

Rate of Incarceration by Nation

Nation	Rate
United States	737
Russia	611
South Africa	335
Israel	209
Mexico	196
England & Wales	148
Australia	126
China	118
Canada	107
Germany	95
France	85
Sweden	82
Japan	62
India	30

incarceration rate
(number of people in prison per 100,000 population)

TAKEN FROM: The Sentencing Project, "New Incarceration Figures: Thirty-three Consecutive Years of Growth," December 2006.

Focusing on the Problems

But Pew rightly points to problems in the nation's imprisonment policy and in what it does (or, typically, doesn't do) to prevent crime in the first place. Take California. It has failed to manage well the health—especially the mental health—problems of many of its inmates. Federal judges are in the process of imposing tough new rules to rectify the problem. Nor has the state found good ways to integrate former inmates back into society. Instead, parole officers routinely send people back to prison if they misbehave—and sometimes the return orders are for minor violations.

California does not handle drug offenders wisely either. Just how big this problem is remains uncertain because some inmates involved in serious crimes plead out to drug offenses to avoid tougher prison sentences. For serious drug users who have not committed a major crime, the goal should be to get them into a community treatment program and keep the offenders there.

To do that, we might emulate the HOPE (Hawaii's Opportunity for Probation with Enforcement) project in Honolulu. The program, started by state Judge Steven Alm in 2004, aims to get probationers to stay in a treatment program. Alm makes offenders take a random, mandatory drug test every week. If they fail, he immediately sends them to jail for a short time to discourage them from being on drugs. Within four years, according to a study by professors Mark Kleiman of UCLA and Angela Hawken of Pepperdine University, the violation rate among HOPE probationers fell by 90%. (Oddly, the Pew report, in discussing our "excessive" use of prison, makes no mention of the fact that there are about as many felons on probation as there are in prison.)

There is more that could be done to prevent young people from embarking on a life of crime. The Pew report rightly notes the success of the High/Scope Perry Preschool Project in Michigan, which began in the 1960s. The project has reduced delinquency among children of (mostly) poor black women by exposing them to a high-quality preschool program.

What we have learned from High/Scope is especially noteworthy because a random sample of youngsters were enrolled in the preschool program and the results were compared with those of a control group.

The Pew report could have mentioned at least 10 other crime-prevention programs that work. They can be found in "Blueprints for Violence Prevention," published by the Institute of Behavioral Science at the University of Colorado, and include Big Brothers/Big Sisters, nurse home-visitation programs and various special education programs in high schools. All were rigorously tested by controlled experiments in at least two locations.

Many Criminals Still Avoid Prison

But even with prevention programs, there will always be many people in prison. A major challenge for scholars today is to discover better ways of placing ex-inmates back into the community. If such methods can be devised, we can reduce the large number of parolees who are sent back to prison for violating the terms of their release.

But we should not suppose that, except for some minor drug offenders, we imprison too many people. There are still people who ought to be in prison and are not. There are more than 1 million felons on probation, in many cases because prisons are overcrowded, according to the Bureau of Justice Statistics. There are violent gang members who are hard to arrest and convict because their neighbors are afraid to go to the police or testify against them.

It is discouraging to read a report by an important private organization that can do no better than say we incarcerate too many people, get nothing from it and are stealing money from higher education.

"As the prison population grows, the ef-fect of this growth on crime is reduced, and can even reach a point where its benefit is reversed."

High Incarceration Rates Do Not Necessarily Decrease Crime Rates

Howard N. Snyder and Jeanne B. Stinchcomb

In the following viewpoint, Howard N. Snyder and Jeanne B. Stinchcomb argue that recent research confirms that increased rates of incarceration do not result in decreased rates of crime. Snyder and Stinchcomb contend that crime rates have not de-creased in recent years and have in some cases increased as a re-sult of the growing number of low-level offenders imprisoned and the longer sentences given to offenders. Howard N. Snyder serves as the director of Systems Research at the National Center for Juvenile Justice. Jeanne B. Stinchcomb is a professor of crimi-nology and criminal justice at Florida Atlantic University and the author of Corrections: Past, Present, and Future.

Howard N. Snyder and Jeanne B. Stinchcomb, "Do Higher Incarceration Rates Mean Lower Crime Rates?" *Corrections Today*, v. 68, no. 6, October 2006, pp. 92–97. Copy-right © 2006 American Correctional Association. Reprinted by permission of the Ameri-can Correctional Association, Alexandria, Va.

As you read, consider the following questions:

1. According to the study by Liedka and colleagues, at what point do further increases in the incarceration rate begin to create an increase in crime?

2. According to the argument by Shepherd, what types of criminals enter prison when the overall prison population is small, and what types of criminals enter prisons when the overall prison population is large?

3. How do longer prison sentences impact the crime rate, according to the authors?

All public policies have an impact—even if it is not always the one that was anticipated or desired. That is because there is no simple cause-and-effect relationship between implementing public policy and achieving its objectives. Even the most apparently straightforward correlations often are more complex upon closer examination. The relationship between incarcerating more offenders and reducing crime rates is one such example.

Offenders are sentenced to prison for a wide variety of reasons, ranging from society's desire for retribution to its belief in rehabilitation. But from a more pragmatic perspective, incarceration is fundamentally designed to make our communities safer—by deterring future violators, incarcerating offenders who may be deterred by a brief stint behind bars or incapacitating those who cannot be deterred. In either case, the ultimate purpose is to improve public safety. This concept suggests that as a society relies more on imprisonment as a response to crime, the amount of crime committed in that society should diminish. In other words, crime rates would be expected to decrease as incarceration rates increase. That is the theory. The question is whether it is also the reality.

The Need to Find or Disprove Correlations

Given the skyrocketing costs of imprisonment, the answer has significant implications for both public policy and fiscal priorities. However, while research studies have for some time explored the relationship between prison and crime rates, their findings have not necessarily been consistent over the years. That does not mean that some studies are "wrong" and others are "right." Nor does it diminish the validity of research or imply that researchers are selectively interpreting data to fit their own predispositions. What it does mean is, first, that differing methods of inquiry can produce differing outcomes, and, second, even using the same methods, findings can change over time as the population being studied and society in general likewise change. Thus, before casting shadows of doubt on conflicting outcomes, it is essential to take a closer look.

That is precisely what the American Society of Criminology's journal, *Criminology and Public Policy*, did several months ago with the publication of a series of three articles, all addressing the question: "Do increases in the prison population reduce crime?" Two of the articles report on new research studies, while the third is an essay reacting to the results. Based on data from the 1970s and 1980s, prior research had generally found that prison growth reduces crime. However, questions have been raised about the logical underpinnings of such findings. In fact, the two new studies have uncovered a somewhat different outcome.

Exhausting the Benefits of Prisons

Using state-level prison and reported crime data from 1972 through 2000, [researchers Raymond] Liedka [and colleagues] found that, surprisingly, the effect of prison growth on crime diminishes as the scale of imprisonment increases. In fact, they determined that when the incarceration rate reaches a certain point (the inflection point), a further increase in prison population actually produces an increase in crime. They placed this inflection point at 3.25 prisoners per 1,000 persons in the general population. Moreover, they conclude that the specific effect of an increasing prison population on crime depends on the level of the prison population when the increase started its upward climb. In other words, did the area already have a high rate of incarceration, which was further intensified by additional prison growth? If so, the impact on crime would be expected to be less than might otherwise occur in an area that started its growth spurt from a lower level of incarceration. A prison population increase in one jurisdiction therefore could have a different effect on crime rates than a similar increase in another jurisdiction.

This also implies that even within the same jurisdiction, similar increases at different points in time may have different effects on crime rates, depending on the level of imprisonment at the time. That is, the prison population might be associated with a decrease in crime rates at one point, but with an increase in crime at another.

No Local-Level Crime Reduction

The second new research study, conducted by [researchers Thomislav] Kovandzic and [Lynne] Vieraitis, is based on county-level data from Florida for the years 1980 through 2000. They argue that while state-level studies of the relationship between changing prison populations and crime are a vast improvement over national-level studies, an even closer analysis at the local level is needed to really understand the impact of incarceration rates on crime. Removing selected offenders from a community should maximize the influence on that community's crime rate, an effect that may be greatly diminished (or even lost) using a larger geographic perspective. Additionally, at the local level, research can better control changes in other factors that influence crime rates, such as trends in community demographics, unemployment, income, poverty and the proportion of female-headed households.

On the basis of that logic, Kovandzic and Vieraitis used data from Florida to determine how changes in the number of

Ever-Increasing Incarceration Rates

How can you tell when a democracy is dead? When concentration camps spring up and everyone shivers in fear? Or is it when concentration camps spring up and no one shivers in fear because everyone knows they're not for "people like us" (in [film director] Woody Allen's marvelous phrase) but for the others, the troublemakers, the ones you can tell are guilty merely by the color of their skin, the shape of their nose or their social class?

Questions like these are unavoidable in the face of America's homegrown gulag archipelago, a vast network of jails, prisons and "supermax" tombs for the living dead that, without anyone quite noticing, has metastasized into the largest detention system in the advanced industrial world. The proportion of the US population languishing in such facilities now stands at 737 per 100,000, the highest rate on earth and some five to twelve times that of Britain, France and other Western European countries or Japan. With 5 percent of the world's population, the United States has close to a quarter of the world's prisoners, which, curiously enough, is the same as its annual contribution to global warming. With 2.2 million people behind bars and another 5 million on probation or parole, it has approximately 3.2 percent of the adult population under some form of criminal-justice supervision, which is to say one person in thirty-two.

Daniel Lazare, The Nation, *August 27, 2007.*

county residents sentenced to prison affected the county's violent and property crime rates. They came to the somewhat startling conclusion that their study found "no support for the 'more prisoners, less crime' thesis." That is not to say that prison growth never reduces crime. They conceded that there may be some effect of prison population growth on crime, but "counties that relied most heavily on imprisonment as a tool of crime control did not as a result experience greater reductions in crime." In essence, there appears to be a point of diminishing returns on prison investments. The crime-control benefits of prison growth declined as a community relied more and more heavily on incarceration.

These results contradict earlier findings and even appear to be counterintuitive at first glance. Within prison walls, staff have known for many years that punishing inmates for an increasingly wide range of misbehavior becomes counterproductive at some point. As this research indicates, a similar concept may be operating on a macro level in free society.

A Change in Inmate Population

In response to the disparities across research studies, [Joanna] Shepherd (2006) has integrated their seemingly inconsistent findings, noting that, when the number of prisoners in the criminal justice system is small, adding additional inmates tends to decrease violent and property crime. However, as the prison population grows, the effect of this growth on crime is reduced, and can even reach a point where its benefit is reversed. Shepherd's argument is based on the fact that different types of offenders enter into confinement when prison populations are small, in contrast to those entering when they are large—that is, the types of offenders entering America's prisons in the 1970s and 1980s were not the same as those entering in the 1990s.

As Shepherd argues, when prison populations were small, additional inmates being admitted tended to be primarily violent and property offenders. It makes sense that removing these offenders would have a direct impact on the rate of violent and property crime in their local communities. However, as prison populations grew in the 1990s, a substantial portion of that growth was a product of the incarceration of drug-related violators and such low-level offenders as probation violators. Confining these offenders may have some impact on local violent and property crime rates, but is destined to produce a smaller effect on these crime rates than the incarceration of violent and property offenders.

As Shepherd speculates, there are a number of reasons why the incarceration of drug-related and low-level offenders would have less ability to reduce official crime rates than the incarceration of violent and property offenders, and, in fact, may even increase these crime rates. For example, disruption of drug markets reduces the supply and increases the cost of drugs, encouraging addicts to commit more crime to support their habit. As illegal drugs become more expensive, there is greater incentive for drug sellers to commit violent crimes to control their more-lucrative markets. Even when drug sellers are forced or frightened out of the drug business, they may move to economic crime. Shepherd is likewise concerned that focusing on drug enforcement may divert scarce resources away from controlling other criminal activities. At the same time, early release programs in response to the pressure of prison crowding may be placing higher-risk offenders back on the street.

Longer Sentences for Lesser Crimes

But it is not only the rate of imprisonment that has an impact; longer prison sentences play a role as well. While length of stay has increased for all offenders in recent years, due to truth-in-sentencing laws, the effect has been greatest on the prison terms of low-level offenders. Lengthening prison terms for these offenders may have no effect on crime, or may even cause crime to increase. As Shepherd speculates, many criminal careers are relatively short, so incapacitating low-level offenders for longer periods may have little crime-reducing influence because they would have largely ended their criminal activities well before their release dates. Moreover, the longer an offender's sentence, the greater the "collateral consequences" of conviction—everything from future employment prospects to family relationships—thereby limiting the offender's non-criminal alternatives after release. Longer terms in prison also give these low-level offenders more opportunity to learn from other inmates. As ironic as it may seem, it may well be true that shorter sentences for low-level offenders would actually reduce crime more than longer sentences; in fact, it is quite possible that the crime-increasing effects of placing more and more drug and low-level offenders in prison may be offsetting the crime-reducing effect of incarcerating more violent and property offenders.

No Simple Solution to Crime Reduction

In contrast to more recent studies, earlier research indicating a link between prison population growth and crime reduction was conducted in an era before the prison net had widened to embrace a larger number and proportion of drug and low-level offenders. As a result of transitions in the nature of the prison population, contemporary prison population growth not only has less influence on violent and property crime rates, it also has led to a series of dynamics that may have actually caused crime to increase in some communities.

Like all other public policies, the trend toward collective incapacitation has had an impact—although, perhaps, not one that was either anticipated or desired. At least in part, that is because [as stated in the book *Corrections: Past, Present, and Future*] "even the best intentions are doomed to failure in the absence of informed decisions based on projections of expected impact." Essentially, sophisticated problems are not solved by simplistic solutions.

> *"The fact is that it is cheaper, in the long-run, to help inmates not return to prison and jail than to keep re-arresting them."*

Comprehensive Reentry Programs Will Reduce Recidivism

Mark A. Nadler

In the following viewpoint, Mark A. Nadler argues for the use of comprehensive reentry programs in jails to reduce recidivism. Nadler emphasizes the importance of teaching inmates the skills needed to establish gainful employment and manage their finances, stating that often having a stable job and income will prevent an ex-offender from returning to crime. Mark A. Nadler is an associate professor of economics at Ashland University in Ohio and is the co-author of Microcomputer Macroeconomics.

As you read, consider the following questions:

1. What percentage of inmates were on probation at the time of arrest, and what percentage had prior sentences, according to a Bureau of Justice Statistics report cited by Nadler?

2. What does Nadler see as some of the tragic consequences of re-arrest rates due to the failure of reentry
efforts?

3. What two conditions does Nadler claim are necessary
for an individual to stay out of jail?

Legislators, community officials, and correction leaders now
recognize the societal costs of our country's high rate of
prison recidivism and the ineffectiveness of current reentry efforts. A high recidivism rate not only translates into thousands of new crimes committed each year but also means that
the public has to spend billions of extra dollars to capture and
reincarcerate the same individuals repeatedly. But this is not
only a dollar issue. Recidivism also adversely impacts public
safety, the welfare of children, family unification, the fiscal
health of our states and communities, and community health.
Forces are mounting nationally to reduce the high rate of recidivism. "But largely missing from the conversation is how
jails can be part of this effort" [states Michelle Gaseau, managing editor of *Corrections.com*].

Jails historically have been repositories for criminals and
social misfits. Jails are mostly locally operated correctional facilities that hold pretrial persons, hold inmates who are sentenced and awaiting transfer to a prison, and confine inmates
sentenced to a short term. Other functions performed by jails
include: house inmates for federal, state, or other authorities
because of crowding; readmit probation, parole, and bail-
bond violators and absconders; temporally detain juveniles
pending their transfer to juvenile authorities; operate
community-based programs as alternatives to incarceration;
release convicted inmates to the community upon completion
of sentence; hold mentally ill persons pending their movement to health facilities, and for various reasons, like protective custody, hold individuals for the military.

In the future jails will continue to serve their traditional
and expanded roles centering on confinement. Looking ahead,

the real question for jails is whether, and to what extent, they should expand their rehabilitative services to participate in efforts to curb recidivism. In many ways this process has already begun: by jail jurisdiction, 55 percent offer secondary education, 70 percent religious and spiritual counseling, 39 percent fee-for-service health care, and 78 percent mental health screening at intake.

New Solutions to Reduce Recidivism

While all of these forms of rehabilitation are important, including the work done in prisons, overwhelming evidence suggests that they are not sufficient to keep people from returning to jail. At the time of arrest [the Bureau of Justice Statistics reports that] over 50 percent of jail inmates were either on probation, parole, or bail bond; close to 75 percent of jail inmates had prior sentences to incarceration or probation; close to 39 percent of jail inmates had 3 or more prior sentences to probation or incarceration; 41 percent of jail inmates had a current or prior violent offense; 46 percent of jail inmates were nonviolent recidivists; and 13 percent of jail inmates had a current or prior drug offense only. This is leading to jail overcrowding—by midyear 2004 jails were operating at 94 percent of capacity—with even worse consequences for families and communities.

Solutions to jail overcrowding often emphasize building bigger jails, improving the efficiency of jail systems so that people spend less time in them, and diversion tactics so that fewer people are ever sent to jail. It would seem natural to want to add to these strategies reentry and transitional programs (sponsored by jails) so that fewer people, once released, return to jail.

Ignoring the potential role that jails can perform in the reentry process is a tragic oversight given the critical importance jails play in our country's overall justice system. In addition to 713,990 inmates held in jails as of midyear 2004, everyone in prison today had to have some contact with a jail. Since jails act as a focal point for prisons why not take advantage of them to begin the rehabilitation process? Quoting Percy Pitzer, retired Warden from the Federal Bureau of Prisons, "the rehabilitation system makes a critical error in not beginning the reentry process the moment someone is booked into a jail." . . .

The Consequences of Failing at Reentry

Reentry is the process of successfully transitioning an individual from incarceration back to the community. Success in this context means, at the very least, not returning to prison or jail. While reentry in some form has existed for as long as correctional facilities have existed, an argument exists whether reentry efforts have ever been successful. The current failure of reentry efforts is well captured by the fact that two out of every three people released from prison are re-arrested within three years of their release.

The consequences of this are tragic and cover public safety concerns, the welfare of children, family unification, government fiscal issues, and community health, in addition to lost national income due to people being in prisons and jails as opposed to working in factories and corporate offices. What is so startling about this failure is that from 1982 to 2002 expenditures on corrections rose from $9 billion to $60 billion with no apparent change in the likelihood of an individual successfully transitioning back to his community (taken from a quote by Rep. Robert Portman that appears in *The National Conference on Offender Reentry*).

The fact is that no one currently has "the solution" to successful reentry. Each jail in developing their own reentry program has to take account of its goals and resource limitations. Nevertheless, a comprehensive model of reentry seems to be emerging that jail managers should be familiar with. . . .

Most jails suffer from certain constraints that limit their ability to engage in a comprehensive reentry effort. This includes their small size, high turnover rates, and the fact that jails only have "inmates for a short period of time and that means whatever interventions they provide—they must be done quickly" [argues Gaseau]. Also, [she states] "much of the money and attention being spent on reentry efforts has focused on those offenders being released in the community from prison. . . ."

An important question that all jails face is where to place their reentry resources? Jails currently emphasize [according to author of *Exploring Jail Operations* Kenneth E. Kerle] education (mostly secondary and basic adult), counseling (mostly religious and drug related), and mental health services (screening at intake and psychotropic medication). Little effort is put into vocational education (6 percent of jails), job seeking (15 percent of jails), or life skills (21 percent of jails). What's surprising about these breakdowns is the overwhelming evidence linking crime and work. [According to *Outside the Walls: A National Snapshot of Community-Based Prisoner Reentry Programs*] "Having a legitimate job lessens the chances of reoffending following release from prison. Also, the higher the wages, the less likely it is that returning prisoners will return to crime." Yet both in terms of vocational education and job seeking skills prisons seem to underinvest.

Additionally, offenders enter jail with financial difficulties and exit jail with financial difficulties. If there is a black hole in jail reentry efforts it is in personal financial education. This topic seems to be on no one's list of jail help programs unless it can be found under life skills. Worldwide there is now a movement to invest in personal financial education for the "average" person. Given the low earnings individuals report before entering jail and the difficulty ex-offenders have obtaining employment upon release it makes sense to develop in jail inmates good money management skills.

Reentry-Centered Criminal Justice

The time has come to shift the traditional defendant/victim criminal justice paradigm to one that recognizes and appreciates the defendant's eventual return to the community. The reentry-centered paradigm seeks to enhance the prospect of individuals, preserve families, and promote community safety.

Overall, defense counsel, prosecutors, and judges should focus on reentry at the outset of the criminal process. The criminal justice system should adopt a forward-looking approach to punishment, one that considers (and lays out) the effects of the punishment on the individual, his or her family, and his or her community. Such an approach would also incorporate ways for the defendant to maintain and/or enhance his or her family ties, which are critical to reentry.

A reentry-centered approach would require these legal actors to be cognizant, at the outset, of the various legal hurdles that would actually or potentially confront the defendant upon reentry and to take the steps specific to their roles that would help the defendant appreciate and work through those hurdles. Thus, prosecutors would be required to consider these hurdles when making charging decisions, as well as to inform defense counsel of their existence. Defense counsel would be required to analyze these hurdles and to both advise and counsel the client accordingly. In addition, defense counsel would be required to coordinate a reentry plan for the client that would ... account for these hurdles. Lastly, judges would be required to consider these legal hurdles when imposing sentences and to waive or modify consequences if, in particular instances, they would be too harsh or unnecessary.

Michael Pinard, Federal Sentencing Reporter, *December 2007.*

Employment Is Essential to Reentry

From an economic perspective, engaging in a criminal act like burglary or drug trafficking is an individual choice based on comparing the benefits and costs of criminal acts with legitimate work options. As evidence suggests, improving inmate job skills, helping inmates find jobs upon release, and increasing inmate wage potential all have a significant impact on recidivism. Unfortunately, jails face many hurdles in helping inmates with job training and post-release employment.

Research indicates that released prisoners have diminished job prospects for secure employment and decent wages throughout their lifetimes. This is due to a myriad of factors including low general education levels, racism, bias against hiring ex-offenders, exclusion from different occupations, and lack of job skills and experience.

One important constraint on the success of any job training program is age. "Despite a great deal of time and effort, work programs [in general] aimed at young men have not proven routinely successful" [states criminologist Shawn Bushway]. An explanation of the age effect offered by Bushway and others is the rather simple observation that before someone desists from crime he must make a . . . decision to stop engaging in criminal behavior. Older offenders benefit from work programs because they make this decision to desist while younger offenders do not. This suggests that with younger inmates investments ought to be made directed at changing their motivation. Bushway, using Job Corps [a free education and vocational training program for people age 16–24, offered by the U.S. Department of Labor] as a model of how to change motivation levels of young people, comes to the conclusion that it is possible to accomplish but very expensive.

Improving the educational levels of inmates and providing inmates with job skills are areas that jails, working with their community services, can accomplish. Jails probably have little or no power in changing mandated exclusions from certain occupations. One area that jails, given their community base, can really help ex-offenders deal with employment is in understanding and overcoming employer hesitancy in hiring offenders. . . .

The Need for Financial Skills

While the reentry and transitional literature emphasizes the importance of ex-offenders finding a stable and adequate source of income, little stress is placed on helping individuals learn to better manage their money. This is a mistake. Law enforcement and community development groups are beginning to teach financial literacy as part of a broad-based program to reduce crime and revitalize depressed communities.

> [Lee Bowman, Chief of Community Affairs at the Federal Deposit Insurance Corporation (FDIC) states] "Financial education is not only the key to helping people enter the financial mainstream and achieve their economic dreams, it also is one answer to the poverty and despair that leads some individuals to turn to crime"

And,

> Tom Stokes, the FDIC's Community Affairs Officer in Atlanta, argues that "financial education can play a role in helping young people in particular steer away from crime. It's the notion of early intervention—of involving them [i.e., young people] in productive activities where they can learn to save money for education or job goals."

Given that many individuals released from jail are going to work in low-wage jobs money management skills are critical for their success. Improving financial skills also positively impacts marital relationships and diminishes adult driven financial frustrations that are often vented against children. . . .

The Five Stages of Employment Reentry Programs

Intake. Upon intake, assess for each individual their employment situation, educational level, literacy, vocational interests, and aptitudes of individuals entering jail.

Jail. Teach inmates skills based on market demand and public safety requirements. Employers want the following work readiness skills: honesty, reliability, punctuality, and [for the worker to] possess a positive attitude toward work. Cognitive skills stressed should include reading, writing, and arithmetic. Evidence [from public policy professor Harry Holzer and colleagues] suggests "that employers are relatively more willing to hire ex-offenders in construction and manufacturing than in retail trade or the services and that willingness to hire them is particularly low in jobs that require a variety of skills or tasks and especially direct contact with customers." Finally, make sure that inmates have their social security card.

Transition. Promote employment of people released from your jail and facilitate the creation of job opportunities. Given the importance of job interviewing and filling out a clean application, especially for smaller companies that use these devices as screens to eliminate unwelcome job applicants, emphasize these skills. Work with various nonprofits and other groups to develop transitional work experiences (3 to 6 months) that prove to an employer the ability of an ex-offender to hold a job in a responsible manner.

Community. Recognize and address those obstacles that make it difficult for someone who has been incarcerated to obtain and retain viable employment while under community supervision. Deal with racism and bias of employers. Educate employers about the limits to their legal liabilities when hiring ex-offenders, and the availability of "bonding" or tax credits from federal and state governments when employing ex-offenders [suggests Holzer].

Service Systems. Create a comprehensive workforce system that is integrated, market driven and accountable. [The *Outside the Walls* report states] "One reason cited for why job training has not been more effective in reducing recidivism is the general lack of job placement assistance and other follow-up after release from prison. This follow-up period may be particularly important for employers who indicate a willingness to hire former prisoners if a third-party intermediary or case manager is available to work with the new hire to help prevent problems. Programs such as these, working with departments of correction or operating as community-based organizations, offer promise in connecting former prisoners to full-time employment and lowering levels of criminal activity and substance abuse."

The Five Stages of Financial Reentry Programs

Intake. Upon incarceration all jail inmates should have a financial background file developed that includes the following: tax compliance status, consumer credit report, Chex-System consumer report, bankruptcy status, child support status, Dun and Bradstreet report for inmates that owned a business, and a check for pending civil litigations that will involve a financial burden upon release.

This information provides a guide for all of the financial issues that need to be resolved before release or the development of a plan that resolves these problems upon release.

Jail. Develop financial literacy with special emphasis on financial goal setting, budgeting, use of legitimate financial institutions like banks, insurance, and saving and investment strategies.

Transition. Construct a two-year personal financial plan that is integrated into a budget that is supportable by the wage the inmate can legitimately earn and available social services.

Community and Service Systems. Set appointments for released inmates with social services and credit counseling agencies. Establish a savings and checking account with a local bank....

High recidivism rates have finally captured the attention of both Democrats and Republicans. The fact is that it is cheaper, in the long-run, to help inmates not return to prison and jail than to keep re-arresting them. This is an argument that seems to have been won. The question then is how to accomplish this goal. While pieces of the solution are evolving, primary focus for dealing with this problem has been with prisons. My argument is that jails have a critical, and maybe the most critical role to play in this process given their unique role as "point men" in the criminal justice system.

While jails have been engaged in reentry efforts, their primary focus, at least statistically, has been on activities other than job placement and financial literacy. I have argued that this is a mistake. My hypothesis is that having a job and learning how to manage money are both necessary conditions for staying out of jail. Evidence in support of the role of work in successfully transitioning out of prison and jail is strong. The role of financial literacy is beginning to become recognized as a necessary ingredient to achieve a stable life. If poverty and its correlates are to be ever reversed then teaching people how to accumulate wealth must be part of the solution.

Jails should begin incorporating into their own mission a plan to help inmates get a job and manage money.

> *"Each failure to enforce treatment re-
> quirements could encourage offenders
> to ignore future service obligations or
> flout future constraints."*

Reentry Programs Are Often Flawed

Douglas B. Marlowe

*In the following viewpoint, Douglas B. Marlowe argues that re-
habilitation programs for prisoners are often developed using unproven and unstandardized techniques. This often results in the
failure of these programs to reduce recidivism in any significant
way, Marlowe asserts. Using the results of a recent intervention
program, Project Greenlight, Marlowe claims that by offering
prisoners multiple methods of rehabilitation, the program places
too much pressure on the inmates, dooming them to failure. According to Marlowe, in order for a rehabilitation program to
succeed, it must offer prisoners clear guidelines and punish them
for failure to comply. Douglas B. Marlowe is director of the Division on Law & Ethics Research at the Treatment Research Institute (TRI), a nonprofit institute dedicated to reducing the effects*

Douglas B. Marlowe, "When 'What Works' Never Did: Dodging the 'Scarlet M' in Correctional Rehabilitation," *Criminology and Public Policy*, vol. 5, no. 2, May 2006, pp.
339–344. Copyright © 2006 American Society of Criminology. All rights reserved. Reproduced by permission.

of drug and alcohol abuse on individuals, and an adjunct profes-
sor of psychology at the University of Pennsylvania.

As you read, consider the following questions:

1. According to the author, why has the field of correctional rehabilitation suffered as a result of downplaying
   or ignoring negative research findings?

2. What percentage of inmates in Project Greenlight par-
   ticipated in family counseling, according to research
   conducted following the completion of the program?

3. How does the absence of follow-through after imprisonment affect inmates, according to Marlowe?

Virtually every article on correctional rehabilitation begins
by reviewing the demise of the "nothing works" philosophy purportedly ushered in by [sociologist Robert] Martinson
(1974). The latent message to other researchers is unmistak-
able: Question the value of offender rehabilitation and risk
similar vilification for apostasy. Being branded with the "Scarlet M" (for Martinson) can have serious repercussions for
one's professional reputation and ability to obtain grant funding or gainful employment.

Because any negative finding could be interpreted as casting pallor on the concept of rehabilitation or could grind a
line of research to a halt, investigators often feel compelled to
declare victory at every turn. If their primary hypotheses are
not confirmed, they can usually rely on post hoc correlations
to elicit some evidence of treatment effects. And if that is insufficient, the failsafe position is to conclude that the intervention might not have been adequately implemented. If we simply do more of the same for a longer period of time, it will
surely succeed.

In the final analysis, this process does a grave disservice to
the field of correctional rehabilitation. The literature is so rife
with "noise" touting unproven interventions that practitioners

and policy makers have difficulty separating the wheat from the chaff. It is difficult to discern which interventions are, in fact, evidence based and worthy of implementation, and which should be consigned to the scrap pile. As a result, the field fails to learn from its mistakes and continuously reinvents unworthy paradigms.

This process was recently manifested in the evaluation of the Project Greenlight Reentry Program for parolees returning to residence in New York City (Wilson and Davis, 2006). After an initial period of in-prison preparatory training, eligible inmates were transferred to a local jail facility where they received eight additional weeks of intensive transitional services designed to connect them to community resources and reconnect them with family members or other social supports. Ostensibly drawing from the "what works" literature, the counseling components of the program were intended to be multimodal [adressing the "modalities" of human beings: think, feel, act, sense, imagine, and interact] and cognitive-behavioral [focusing on individuals' thoughts in order to modify feelings and behavior] in orientation, and to include family therapy, job-readiness, and substance abuse treatment services.

Contrary to expectations, in a quasi-experimental design, it was found that [the 344] inmates attending this program had higher rates of criminal recidivism and parole revocations than two comparable groups [made up of 278 and 113] inmates assigned to parole as usual. Moreover, despite receiving significantly more treatment services, they reaped no benefits on proximal outcomes, including employment, family relationships, engagement in community activities, or compliance with parole conditions. . . . Characterizing these findings as "unexpected and puzzling," [rather than attributing them to the treatment program itself] the investigators concluded they could have been attributable to the relatively abbreviated length of the intervention. Coerced treatment might elicit feelings of resistance, resentment, or confusion on the part of offenders in the short term, which could take a longer time to resolve. Perhaps administering the same or a similar program for a longer interval of time would counteract these short-term negative reactions and produce long-term gains.

An alternative explanation is that the developers of Project Greenlight were misled by the "what works" literature into adopting inert or counter-productive program elements. A closer look at the research evidence raises serious questions of whether various components of Project Greenlight were justified from the outset.

Where Was the Evidence?

The counseling platform for Project Greenlight was derived from the Reasoning and Rehabilitation (R&R) Program (Ross and Fabiano, 1985). Conceived in Canada, this cognitive-behavioral curriculum presumes that criminal activity is often mediated by impulsive, rigid, and egocentric thinking. The goal, therefore, is to assist offenders to forestall impulsive action in favor of productive thought. Offenders are taught to anticipate the consequences of their actions, consider alternative courses of action, and contemplate the impact of their conduct on other people (i.e., develop empathy and perspective-taking).

Unfortunately, research provides lackluster support for this intervention. A recent quantitative review (Wilson et al., 2005a) concluded that outcomes for R&R were mixed across studies, with an overall mean effect size (ES) of 0.16. This effect is small and translates into a reduction of only a few percentage-points in recidivism. Similar findings were reported (Lipsey et al., 2001) in an earlier meta-analysis, in which most ES's for R&R were determined to be statistically nonsignificant and small in magnitude. Factor in the well-known "publication bias," in which negative findings are systematically screened out of the research literature (e.g. Mc-

Cord, 2003), and the actual effect size could be expected to range somewhere between statistically nonsignificant and clinically irrelevant. Consider further the placebo effects and novelty effects that often give an unwarranted boost in research studies to behavioral interventions, which cannot be administered double-blind, and the true effect size is apt to be negligible.

Importantly, much formative research on R&R involved single-group, pre-to-post designs that focused predominantly on self-report, attitudinal measures of outcomes (Correctional Service of Canada, 2001). Such designs are so seriously biased in favor of an intervention (e.g. Weisburd et al., 2001) that they were not included in the meta-reviews of R&R just mentioned. Moreover, the sample sizes in the formative studies often numbered in the thousands, which would have enabled the investigators to detect statistical significance with small effects.

Project Greenlight further incorporated elements of the transtheoretical stages-of-change model (McConnaughy et al., 1983). This paradigm involves matching clients to interventions based on an assessment of their readiness to change problem behaviors, which is theorized to fall along a continuum of successive stages of motivation. For example, individuals who are "pre-contemplative" of change (that is, unmotivated) would be matched to a motivational-enhancement intervention, whereas those who are in "preparation" or "action" for change would be matched to a behavioral or cognitive-behavioral intervention involving proactive therapeutic strategies.

Although the stages-of-change model has intuitive appeal and makes a good deal of logical sense, it has minimal empirical support. Psychometric studies have consistently failed to confirm the hypothesized factor structure for the stages of change (Carey et al., 1999; Sutton, 2001; West, 2005), and meta-reviews have found no evidence to suggest that stage-based interventions produce better outcomes than non-stage-based interventions, usual-care treatment, or no treatment (Project MATCH Research Group, 1997; Riemsma et al., 2002).

Failing in Counseling and Vocational Training

Project Greenlight also provided family counselors who sought to connect inmates with social support networks and conducted therapy groups with inmates and their relatives or significant others. The counseling paradigm used for the family-based interventions is vaguely articulated in the descriptive literature on Project Greenlight; however, it seems to have been derived largely from a social work model that focused on marshalling community resources and problem-solving hurdles to reentry (Bobbitt and Nelson, 2004).

Unfortunately, family counseling interventions of this ilk have rarely been studied in controlled clinical evaluations. Meta-analyses and review articles have failed to uncover support for their effectiveness. To the contrary, the overarching conclusion from research reviews is that family interventions incorporating behavioral-contracting or reinforcement-training techniques are the only ones to show reliable evidence of efficacy for adult identified clients (e.g. Fals-Stewart and Birchler, 2001; Moyers and Hester, 1999; O'Farrell, 1993). Non-behavioral family interventions such as those apparently used in Project Greenlight have no evidence of efficacy.

Finally, Project Greenlight provided pre-vocational, job-readiness training. This four-week course taught inmates how to search for a job, interview for a job, and behave appropriately while on the job. Again, although such an approach has intuitive appeal, little evidence supports its utility. The research literature on pre-vocational interventions has been plagued by serious methodological shortcomings, poorly defined and non-standardized interventions, and imprecise criteria for success (Magura et al., 2004). Only a few interven-

Acknowledging the Challenges of Prisoner Rehabilitation

The individuals incarcerated in U.S. juvenile and adult prisons have multiple deficiencies and problems likely to hinder their ability to successfully transition from institution to a crime-free life in the community. As detailed by many researchers, these deficiencies include little education, few job skills, little job experience likely to lead to good employment, substance and alcohol dependency, and other health problems, including mental health problems. . . .

What is less often acknowledged and discussed is that these returning inmates have already been through (having failed or been failed by) the other social and public institutions and agencies designed to produce good citizens. In particular, many of those who end up incarcerated did poorly in the school systems that provide educational foundations for a successful adulthood. Many offenders have histories of abuse and neglect and may have been referred to, or in the custody of, family and social services. Adult inmates often have histories of juvenile confinement and adult probation that failed to provide the services, programming and support to reform and rehabilitate. And finally, many inmates have received alcohol and drug treatment outside the criminal justice system, but may remain addicted to drugs and alcohol. At this point, responsibility for helping these offenders become productive citizens is handed to underfunded agencies whose primary responsibility is public safety—not rehabilitation.

Pamela K. Lattimore, Corrections Today, *April 2007.*

tions—for example, the Job Seekers Workshop (Hall et al., 1985) and Vocational Problem-Solving (Metzger et al., 1992)—

have been identified as showing promise in the research literature. Importantly, these are manualized interventions that require substantial training and supervision of counselors as well as ongoing fidelity monitoring of the protocol to be effective, which does not seem to have been incorporated into Project Greenlight (Wilson et al., 2005b). Moreover, under controlled research conditions, these interventions have not always shown evidence of efficacy and have been known to suffer from unacceptably high attrition rates and inattention from clients (Lidz et al., 2004).

In summary, Project Greenlight seems to have delivered a hodgepodge of unproven and unstandardized clinical interventions, which could explain why it failed to produce positive effects on virtually any outcome measure. A more difficult question, however, is why [the program itself might produce negative] effects. No compelling evidence links these counseling interventions to harmful influences on clients. It would seem that providing a menu of inconsequential services is more than simply wasteful and inefficient. If the services lack appreciable credibility, this might imbue clients with a sense of futility, prime them to reject future services, or inure them against the active ingredients of successful programs. If so, then providing weak treatments could, under some circumstances, be worse than providing no treatment at all.

Where Was the Credibility?

Most criminal offenders are knee-jerk skeptics. Their histories are often littered with would-be caregivers rendering superficial aid, failing to set responsible limits on their conduct, and fading from view before achieving meaningful gains. Reenacting this process simply demonstrates that their jaded expectations are justified and may make them less likely to trust future overtures of assistance, which could explain why a history of previous treatment episodes has been paradoxically associated in some studies with negative outcomes in correctional rehabilitation programs (e.g. Marlowe et al., 2003). Each disappointing episode might undermine offenders' confidence in professionals and generate counterproductive feelings of pessimism or despondency. Moreover, each failure to enforce treatment requirements could encourage offenders to ignore future service obligations or flout future constraints.

The participants in Project Greenlight were generally noncompliant with treatment services. For instance, only about 30% of the inmates (105 out of 344) agreed to participate in family counseling and only about 15% (50 out of 344) attended a single family session (Bobbitt and Nelson, 2004). What consequences, if any, were incurred by those who were planning to reside with relatives or significant others, but failed to follow through with family counseling requirements? If familial interactions are hypothesized to influence success on parole, then rejection of family counseling—either by the inmates, their significant others, or both—should have been viewed as a negative risk factor for recidivism or technical violations. Perhaps release on parole should, therefore, have been made contingent upon completion of the full sequence of family counseling obligations.

It was further noted in the evaluation that many participants were "unengaged" in the cognitive-behavioral counseling sessions and many of them angrily insisted they did not require substance abuse treatment (Wilson and Davis, 2006). To be conducted competently, cognitive-behavioral counseling requires active engagement during in-session activities plus the completion of an ongoing sequence of "homework assignments." Were there consequences for failing to follow through with the assignments, and were participants' assertions of sobriety confirmed by urine drug-screens and breathalyzer testing? If not, outcomes should be expected to be poor on the whole. Worse still, failing to respond to this nonfeasance may have inadvertently communicated the message to participants that other obligations, including parole requirements, are similarly "optional" and can be ignored with impunity. This message could very well have elicited a paradoxical reaction and made outcomes worse than if no services had been offered in the first instance.

After their release from detention, the participants in Project Greenlight did receive more treatment services than the comparison subjects. However, these statistically significant differences were small in magnitude (1.23 vs. 0.51 service contacts on average) (Wilson and Davis, 2006). Given the high probability that the inmates had a range of dire service needs, either they failed to follow through with treatment referrals or few services were available in the community to satisfy their needs. Either way, the absence of follow-through after imprisonment reflects poor clinical practice and is apt to have confirmed the inmates' worst suspicions that they cannot rely on professionals to assist them over the long haul. Indeed, failing to live up to this promise may have evoked worse outcomes than if no promise had ever been made.

Conclusion

"Kitchen sink" interventions are usually bad practice and ill-advised policy because they place unwarranted demands on participants and on system resources. Most offenders are characteristically irresponsible and have considerable difficulty satisfying basic obligations. It defies logic to expect that increasing the dosage of ineffective treatments would improve their outcomes. This course of action would be most likely to overburden participants, interfere with their engagement in productive activities, and drain precious resources from effective programs.

It makes the least sense to offer an expensive and fragmented menu of interventions to offenders, from which they are permitted to pick and choose whether to show up for the sessions or pay attention. The truth is that it would represent considerable incremental gains for many offenders if they simply made it to counseling sessions on time and completed relevant homework assignments. At a minimum, therefore, release on parole should be made explicitly contingent upon inmates showing up for their scheduled appointments, paying attention to the discussions, completing the required exercises, and demonstrating proficiency on and understanding of the concepts. Furthermore, continuance on parole should be contingent upon following through with reasonable post-prison treatment referrals. Failing to hold offenders accountable for such basic obligations unacceptably lowers expectations for them and permits them to cycle downward in a continued pattern of recklessness and immaturity. This conclusion is not the same as saying that nothing works for offenders, although some critics might be tempted to attach the "Scarlet M" to such a position. Perhaps an "R" (for realistic) would be a fairer characterization.

References

Bobbitt, Michael and Marta Nelson, 2004, The Front Line: Building Programs that Recognize Families' Role in Reentry. New York: Vera Institute of Justice.

Carey, Kate B., Daniel M. Purnine, Stephen A. Maisto, and Michael P. Carey, 1999, Assessing readiness to change substance abuse: A critical review of instruments. Clinical Psychology: Science & Practice 6:245-266.

Correctional Service of Canada, 2001, Evaluation of the Correctional Service of Canada substance abuse programs: OSAAP, ALTO, and choices. Ottawa, Ont.: Available at: http://www.csc-scc.gc.ca/text/pblct/forum/e133/e1331_e.shtml (Accessed February 21, 2006).

Fals-Stewart, William and Gary R. Birchler, 2001, A national survey of the use of couples therapy in substance abuse treatment. Journal of Substance Abuse Treatment 20:277-283.

Hall, S.M., P. Loeb, and M. LeVois, 1985, Job Seekers' Workshop: Leader's Manual for a Vocational Rehabilitation Program. Bethesda, Md.: National Institute on Drug Abuse.

Lidz, Victor, Diane M. Sorrentino, Lenore Robison, and Scott Bunce, 2004, Learning from disappointing outcomes: An evaluation of prevocational interventions for methadone maintenance patients. Substance Use & Misuse 39:2287-2308.

Lipsey, Mark W., G.L. Chapman, and N.A. Landenberger, 2001, Cognitive-behavioral programs for offenders. Annals of the American Academy of Political and Social Science 578:144-157.

Magura, Stephen, Graham L. Staines, Laura Blankertz, and Elizabeth M. Madison, 2004, The effectiveness of vocational services for substance users in treatment. Substance Use & Misuse 39:2165-2213.

Marlowe, Douglas B., Nicholas S. Patapis, and David S. Dematteo, 2003, Amenability to treatment of drug offenders. Federal Probation, 67:40-46.

Martinson, Robert, 1974, What works? Questions and answers about prison reform. The Public Interest 35:22-54.

McConnaughy, E.A., James O. Prochaska, and Wayne F. Velicer, 1983, Stages of change in psychotherapy: Measurement and sample profiles. Psychotherapy: Theory, Research and Practice 20: 368-375.

McCord, J., 2003, Cures that harm: Unanticipated outcomes of crime prevention programs. Annals of the American Academy of Political and Social Science 587:16-30.

Metzger, D. S., J.J. Platt, D. Zanis, and I. Fureman, 1992, Vocational Problem Solving: A Structured Intervention for

Unemployed Substance Abuse Treatment Clients. Philadelphia, Penn.: Institute for Addictive Disorders, Drexel University College of Medicine.

Moyers, T. and R.K. Hester, 1999, Outcomes Research: Alcoholism. In M. Galanter and H.D. Kleber (eds.), Textbook of Substance Abuse Treatment. 2d ed. Washington, D.C.: American Psychiatric Press.

O'Farrell, T.J., 1993, Treating Alcohol Problems: marital and Family Interventions. New York: Guilford Press.

Project MATCH Research Group, 1997, Matching treatments to client heterogeneity: Project MATCH postreatment outcomes. Journal of Studies on Alcohol 58:7-29.

Riemsma, Robert P., Jill Pattenden, Christopher Bridle, Amanda J. Sowden, Lisa Mather, Ian S. Watt, and Anne Walker, 2002, A systematic review of the effectiveness of interventions based on a stages-of-chance approach to promote behaviour change. Health Technology Assessment 6.

Ross, R.R. and E.A. Fabiano, 1985, Time to Think: A Cognitive Model of Delinquency Prevention and Offender Rehabilitation. Johnson City, Tenn.: Institute of Social Sciences and Arts.

Sutton, Stephen, 2001, Back to the drawing board? A review of applications of the transtheoretical model to substance abuse. Addiction 96:175-186.

Weisburd, David, Cynthia M. Lum, and Anthony Petrosino, 2001, Does research design affect study outcomes in criminal justice? Annals of the American Academy of Political and Social Science 578:50-70.

West, Robert, 2005, Time for a chance: Putting the transtheoretical (stages of change) model to rest. Addiction 100:1036-1039.

Wilson, David B., Leanna A. Bouffard, and Doris L. MacKenzie, 2005a, A quantitative review of structured, group-oriented, cognitive-behavioral programs for offenders. Criminal Justice & Behavior 32:172-204.

Wilson, James A., Yury Cheryachukin, Robert C. Davis., Jean Dauphinee, Robert Hope, Kajal Gehi, and Timothy Ross, 2005b, Smoothing the Path from Prison to Home: A summary. New York: Vera Institute of Justice.

Wilson, James A. and Robert C. Davis, 2006, Good intentions meet hard realities: An evaluation of the Project Greenlight Reentry Program. Criminology & Public Policy. This issue.

> *"Faith-based prison programs should be widely permitted and encouraged, largely unfettered by secular administrators and counselors."*

Faith-Based Prison Rehabilitation Programs Should Be Supported by the Government

John D. Hewitt

In the following viewpoint, John D. Hewitt contends that faith-based prison rehabilitation programs should be supported by the government because they offer inmates the ability to change their lives for the better and therefore benefit society as a whole. He believes that support of faith-based programs should not be dependent upon the presentation of empirical evidence because their positive impact cannot always be measured by science. Finally he argues that, when considering the integration of faith-based programs into prisons, providing prisoners an opportunity to experience the grace and redemption of God trumps the question of whether federal funds should be used in support of reli-

John D. Hewitt, "Having Faith in Faith-Based Prison Programs," *Criminology and Public Policy*, vol. 5, no. 3, August 2006, pp. 551–556. Copyright © 2006 American Society of Criminology. All rights reserved. Reproduced by permission.

gious programs. John D. Hewitt is a professor of criminal justice at Grand Valley State University in Michigan and the co-author of Delinquency in Society.

As you read, consider the following questions:

1. According to Hewitt, what is problematic about the current body of research on faith-based rehabilitation programs' impact on prison adjustment and recidivism?
2. How does Hewitt use the Misfit in Flannery O'Connor's short story "A Good Man Is Hard to Find" to support his argument?
3. What policy recommendations does the author make for faith-based prison rehab programs?

Scott Camp et al. (2006) identify factors associated with inmates who volunteer to participate in a faith-based prison program and suggest that knowledge of such factors may help us to understand better the differences in prison outcomes, including prison adjustment and post-release success. The most important distinguishing characteristic seems to be that participants are likely to be "seekers" or inmates who have typically only begun their faith journey since entering prison. Camp et al. also seem to suggest that faith-based programs are not only more attractive to seekers, but also that future research might demonstrate that these programs facilitate participating seekers in experiencing more positive prison outcomes. Research confirming the effects of faith-based programs would then provide support for expansion of these programs.

But reading the findings from their study, as well as those of related studies, left me curious about the larger body of social science research into the relationship of religion and faith, crime and delinquency, and faith-based programming aimed at either facilitating or strengthening an individual's faith to help prevent crime or to lower recidivism. Can social science actually lead us to effective policies in this arena? Is it possible to build public policy on a foundation that cannot be scientifically examined and established? The rapidly growing body of literature on the impact of religion or religious participation on prison adjustment and recidivism seems somewhat problematic. The most critical problem seems to reside in the nature and obvious limits of the research. These studies, based largely on survey data or personal observations and anecdotal evidence, all suffer the common inability to tap the personal *internal* changes in inmates.

In 1976, Charles (Chuck) Colson [chief counsel for President Richard Nixon] published his first book, *Born Again*, in which he describes his fall from power and influence in the White House and eventual incarceration in a federal prison. The key factor in the book, however, is not his fall, but his conversion and redemption experience while in prison. Accounts of prison and jailhouse conversions have been widely disseminated and read by the faithful and skeptics alike. The truth or reality of the conversion experience gets debated in the media, among lawmakers, and by the public. Sometimes a conversion experience makes it to the U.S. Supreme Court. In 1981, William Payton was tried and convicted of a brutal rape and murder. During the penalty phase, his defense attorney focused on Payton's conversion and commitment to God that had occurred during the year and a half he spent in jail awaiting trial and argued that this should be considered by the jury to be a mitigating circumstance in their deliberations. The prosecutor, however, incorrectly told the jury that California law prohibited them from considering anything that happened after the crime and that they should disregard his conversion. The judge instructed the jury that the prosecutor's statements were merely argument, but he did not tell them the prosecutor was incorrect. The jury found special circumstances in the crime and returned a verdict recommending a death sentence, which the judge then imposed. The California Supreme Court affirmed the sentence, and Payton appealed to the Ninth Circuit Court of Appeals, which overturned the California Court's decision, arguing that the prosecutor's statements may have misled the jury. The case was then appealed to the U.S. Supreme Court, which in 2005 reversed the Ninth Court's ruling, thus allowing the original sentence to be enforced. Part of the argument by the U.S. Supreme Court was that "it was not unreasonable to find that the jurors did not likely believe Payton." Apparently, they were not offered empirical proof of his conversion. But what proof could have been offered? Could social scientists have confirmed his conversion or the conversion of others?

Payton is only one of several recent cases in which inmates facing the death penalty have provided accounts of conversion experiences. What do we make of them? Are these conversion experiences real? Was there a moment of true grace and redemption (a reconciliation to one's salvation that would lead the person away from sin and crime) involving an inmate facing execution? Because it is impossible to confirm or deny scientifically such a conversion experience, the conversion is regarded as something unverifiable, and the execution proceeds. Is this good law or policy?

In Flannery O'Connor's short story, "A Good Man is Hard to Find" (1955), O'Connor describes the moment of possible grace and redemption the Misfit (an escaped murderer) faces. The Misfit may be what Camp et al. (2006) refers to as a seeker, a person just beginning to look through the window at a possible religious experience. The Misfit has actually been obsessed with religion but cannot bring himself to act on the notion that Jesus is the Christ. Consequently, he believes there is "no pleasure but meanness," which is a not uncommon criminal stance. However, at the end of the story, the Misfit, having just murdered five family members on vacation, glimpses momentarily the power of God to redeem him just as he shoots and kills the grandmother. O'Connor seems to be suggesting that a person may be likely to commit crimes, even horrific ones, to test the no-pleasure-but-meanness world view. Would a criminologist have been able to provide scientific evidence of the Misfit's experience? Might demographic and other social data on inmates experiencing conversions or criminals like the Misfit facing but then rejecting Christ really tell us much on which to develop policies or establish programs? Can we measure ethical or moral reform or redemption in terms of transcendent reality (a belief in something beyond life with which we must reckon)? We can measure criminal acts or the absence of criminal acts over a period of time for particular individuals, but can we accurately tap into the deeper religious dimensions of that person's motivations?

The problems social scientists run into in studying faith-based prison programs are not much different from those who attempt to study evil from a scientific perspective. Evil, like faith, is beyond empirical explanation, although numerous social correlates of both evil and faith can be tentatively measured. According to [Virginia Commonwealth University research associate] Thomas Kubarych (2005), evil reflects non-empirical value judgments. Others, such as [psychiatrist] M. Scott Peck (1983), suggest that even though evil includes such things as intentional harms, the use of overt or covert coercion against others, the destruction of both corporeal life and the human spirit, and even narcissistic personality disorders, we still are ultimately unable to apply rigorous scientific research to its true nature.

Paul Knepper [lecturer in social policy at the University of Sheffield] (2003), writing in an earlier issue of this journal, suggests that the exercise of faith is not just another social institution and that an explanation of how social control is exerted by or through faith requires a metaphysical examination, rather than a scientific one. Can social scientists move beyond thinking about faith as little more than another mechanism of social control or as a social variable to be manipulated for the

An Inmate's Suggestions for Prison Theology

What neither a prison ministry nor a prison theology can do is solve the problem of crime or eliminate from society the criminal mind. Such a goal ought not direct prison theology. The goal, rather, must be to bring healing, comfort, renewal, strength, purpose, humanity to one person at a time through an awakened awareness of God. Jesus always dealt with individuals. Jesus taught crowds but he touched individuals. Where I am in prison, I find myself in fellowship with a large number of women, each of whom is an individual person. . . . We have to come up with a healing Word that touches to each of these in a real way—something that is meaningful and compelling for them. . . .

I think prison theology should lead to a creative response to life. It should demand involvement and commitment and responsibility in the business of living. It should use: art therapy, music, story telling, laughter, fun, poetry, drama, volunteering with others, food, community service, victim reconciliation, family mediation, journaling, parenting, gardening; it should deal with the reality of sexuality and the need for healthy choices.

The pressing drive of my prison theology is to discover our best selves and open ourselves to the process of rebuilding the inner person in that image.

Elizabeth Haysom,
Dialog: A Journal of Theology,
Summer 2007.

sake of public policy? Knepper argues that an evidence-based approach to faith-based programs and interventions, claiming objectivity and refusing to specify whether religion is true or false, eventually leads to "an argument for the irrelevance of moral beliefs in human activity" (Knepper, 2003:343). It may well be, as Knepper contends, that policy makers might do better to seek out the observations and beliefs of the faithful themselves, rather than relying on an "intellectual narrow-mindedness that might be best described as *academic fundamentalism*" (italics in original) (Knepper, 2003: 347).

Faith, grace, and redemption are notions poorly understood by secular social scientists. Even social scientists of faith too easily compartmentalize their desire to adhere to the rigors of the scientific method and seem to forget that the practice of religion involves much more than measurable expressions of faith (i.e., church attendance, reading the Bible or other religious tracts, or adherence to particular commonly held religious beliefs). Yet the faithful, as well as seekers progressing toward belief, also have little understanding of exactly how faith works. *Not* being able to understand fully is an essential element of faith, and as Knepper (2003:342) suggests, "social scientists cannot know more about any social activity than the participants themselves."

Positive change, even redemptive change, within the individual inmate, whether brought about by traditional rehabilitative treatment techniques or a religious conversion experienced by a seeker participating in a faith-based prison program, is obviously a desired outcome for those we incarcerate. Such change might, but does not necessarily, lead to a reduced inclination to commit new crimes. This stems in part from the sociolegal construction of crime, which is often, but not always, related to notions of morality. Changes in the moral character of an inmate as the result of participation in a faith-based program may not be sufficient to overcome the overwhelming social, economic, and biosocial forces that contribute to individual criminality.

More importantly, a religious conversion of a "seeker" while in prison, at least a Christian conversion experience, is only the beginning of change in a person. The notion of being "born again" comes from the Bible. In John 3:3, Jesus teaches, "Unless one is born again, he cannot see the kingdom of God." In 1 Peter 2:1–2 we read: "Therefore, putting aside all malice and all guile and hypocrisy and envy and all slander, like newborn babes, long for the pure milk of the word, that by it you may grow in respect to salvation." Rebirth is only the start of learning about grace and how faith may work in one's life. Although the inmate has accepted forgiveness and begins to walk down the path of change, it could be years before there is sufficient clarity in his or her salvation to notice measurable change in behavior. However, even if these internal changes fail significantly to reduce recidivism or immediately correct an inmate's behavioral problems while in prison, they are likely to have profound impact on the person, but again in ways social scientists may find impossible actually to measure.

Do the limitations of social science to measure grace, redemption, and salvation that may occur in prisoners mean that we should not support faith-based programs or even expand their availability in prison? Of course not. The argument I am presenting here is that faith in faith-based prison programs has been incorrectly tied to empirical findings from social science, rather than to the true redemptive changes that occur in the lives of many participants in the programs. Funding for faith-based prison programs, as well as for faith programs in the community, should be provided because offenders or would-be offenders are given opportunities through these programs to have their lives affected and redirected through grace. Rather than make funding available based on positive findings from research, support should be extended because we have faith in these programs and their ability to provide the possibilities of redemptive change.

Should social scientists *not* apply their research tools to the study of religion and faith? On the contrary. As a criminologist I have great faith in the ability of social science to explore and explain much of our social world, especially the observable behaviors and expressed attitudes of people of different faiths. Yet as a person of faith, I strongly believe that grace and redemption are well beyond the reaches of scientific inquiry. I believe faith-based prison programs give correctional administrators one more element for bringing about change in the lives of inmates held in their care.

On a practical basis, what kind of policy recommendations might emerge from this perspective? I would argue that although corrections is administratively the business of the state, and one could therefore argue that it is a secular activity, radical change within an inmate held by the state may be better viewed as a personal commitment. In practice, inmates are subjected to various forms and degrees of punishments and treatments while in prison. Traditionally, treatments have been at the hands of secular psychologists and counselors, operating well removed from the potential of religious intervention. And as [scholar] C. S. Lewis notes (1970:293), many of those in the field of psychology regard religion as a neurosis. Lewis goes on to imply that the practice of correctional reform and its emphasis on secular change is largely misguided. According to Lewis (pp. 292–293):

> The practical problem of Christian politics is not that of drawing up schemes for a Christian society, but that of living as innocently as we can with unbelieving fellow-subjects under unbelieving rulers who will never be perfectly wise and good and who will sometimes be very wicked and very foolish.

If Lewis is correct, then it might behoove us to develop correctional policies that recognize the fully legitimate role of religion and religious programming in state-managed prison systems. It should not be a question of using federal tax dollars to "support" religious enterprises. Instead, we should embrace the potential of what those of faith might bring into our prisons. Radical change, conversion, grace, and redemption are not tools of the state, but they are real forces that work in the lives of people. Faith-based prison programs should be widely permitted and encouraged, largely unfettered by secular administrators and counselors, and permitted to provide the opportunity for offenders to experience the power of God to redeem. Not all will accept the grace and redemption God offers, but we should do all we can to ensure the opportunity for such offers to be made.

One last policy issue needs to be addressed, and it has to do with how the state should respond to offenders who have had conversion experiences while in prison. Should an inmate have a reduced sentence, gaining early release based on our faith in his or her redemption? Should William Payton or other inmates on death row have their death sentences commuted because they testify to encounters with grace? I would argue that decisions about state-imposed sentences should not be tied to inmates' participation in faith-based prison programs or to behavioral changes in participants as a part of their faith journeys, except as those same behaviors would also determine policy with regard to the treatment given nonbelievers.

In the final moments of "A Good Man is Hard to Find," the grandmother finds grace just before she is shot and dies. Grace and redemption do not preclude facing physical punishment and death. Decisions about sentencing and its reductions or commutations are not in the realm of faith. In Matthew 22:21, Christ says, "Render unto Caesar that which is Caesar's; render unto God that which is God's." Sentencing is the province of the state, and conversion experiences should not be used to seek changes in sentences. Incarcerating or executing an offender should be tied to questions of innocence and guilt. Good conduct and early release are also matters of state policy determined by observable behavior—available to nonbelievers as well as believers. People of faith commit crimes, and criminals sometimes become people of faith. Faith-based prison programs should not become involved in managing Caesar's policies on crime and punishment. But Caesar also should not interfere with opportunities for offenders to find grace.

References

Brown v. Payton, 346 F.3d 1204 (2005)

Camp, Scott, Jody Klein-Saffran, Okyun Kwon, Dawn Dagget, and Victoria Joseph, 2006, An exploration into participation in a faith-based prison program. Criminology & Public Policy. This issue.

Colson, Charles, 1976, Born Again. Old Tappan, NJ.: Chosen Books, Inc.

Knepper, Paul, 2003, Faith, public policy, and the limits of social science. Criminology & Public Policy 2:331-352.

Kubarych, Thomas, 2005, On studying evil. Philosophy, Psychiatry & Psychology 12:265-269.

Lewis, C.S., 1970, The Humanitarian Theory of Punishment. In Walter Hooper (ed.), God in the Dock: Essays on Theology and Ethics. Grand Rapids, Mich.: Eerdmans Publishing.

O'Conner, Flannery, 1955 A Good Man is Hard to Find. In Flannery O'Connor, A Good Man is Hard to Find and Other Stories. New York: Harcourt Brace & Company.

Peck, M. Scott, 1983, People of the Lie: The Hope for Healing Human Evil. New York: Touchstone.

> *"All faith-based programs for prison inmates to which state revenue is distributed . . . are an egregious constitutional violation."*

Faith-Based Prison Rehabilitation Programs Are Unconstitutional

Lawrence T. Jablecki

In the following viewpoint, Lawrence T. Jablecki critiques faith-based prison rehabilitation programs, claiming that they are both unfair and unconstitutional. The author argues that these programs are unfair because often only low-level drug offenders are allowed to participate, and prisoners who agree to participate in Christian activities often receive preferential treatment when it comes time to grant parole. Furthermore, he contends that these programs violate constitutional separation of church and state because federal funding, directly or indirectly, supports them. Lawrence T. Jablecki served as director of the Brazoria County Community Supervision and Corrections Department in Angleton, Texas, for eighteen years and taught philosophy at Rice University in Texas.

Lawrence T. Jablecki, "A Critique of Faith-Based Prison Programs," *Humanist*, vol. 65, no. 5, September/October 2005, pp. 11–16. Copyright © 2005 American Humanist Association. Reproduced by permission of the author.

As you read, consider the following questions:

1. According to Jablecki, what types of prisoners are excluded from participating in the faith-based program at the Carol Vance prison unit in Texas?

2. What must the inmates in Chuck Colson's faith-based programs commit to before being allowed to participate in reintegration activities, according to the author?

3. Based on the article by Mark A.R. Kleiman cited by Jablecki, why does the Vance faith-based prison unit appear to have such a high rate of success?

"Faith-based prisons" are the latest fad in a significant number of states' criminal justice systems, and their growth is an egregious threat to the constitutional democracy that George W. Bush, upon ascending to the U.S. presidency, swore to defend and protect. These programs are supported by state revenue distributed directly or indirectly to sectarian religious organizations for the ostensible goals of rehabilitation and reduction of recidivism. And Bush's commitment to such a theologically driven and pessimistic view of the impotency of government to cure our nation's social ills is allowing the continuation of enormous harm to the public interest.

Roots of Faith-based Prison Programs

During his tenure as Texas governor, Bush spawned the "faith-based agenda"—his plan to cure the United States' social ills through the ministries of religious organizations. It started in 1996 when he appointed a sixteen-member Governor's Advisory Task Force on Faith-Based Community Service Groups. The product of this group was a report called *Faith in Action: A New Vision for Church-State Cooperation in Texas*. The following year Bush used this document to justify establishing "The Inner Change Freedom Initiative" program in the Carol Vance prison unit, a male facility of the Texas Department of Criminal Justice.

This program was the brainchild of Chuck Colson, the Watergate convict-cum-evangelical Christian and founder of Prison Fellowship Ministries. A concise statement of the substance of this program in the February 2003 evaluation report of the Texas Criminal Justice Policy Council states:

> The program was designed to facilitate the life transformation of the member eliminating the thinking process which resulted in his incarceration and to rebuild the member's value system, establishing a solid foundation for productive growth ... a three phase program involving prisoners in 16 to 24 months of in-prison biblical programming and 6–12 months of aftercare while on parole. The different program phases focus on biblical education, life skills, community service, leadership and personal faith.

The report further reveals that the initial project involved approximately two hundred beds in a separate wing of the Vance Unit. No sex offenders, murderers, or inmates convicted of aggravated assault were allowed to volunteer for the program. The outcome of this highly restrictive list of eligibility criteria was that the participants were basically medium- to low-risk drug offenders. In April 1997 the initial group of 141 volunteers "hand selected" by administrators of Colson's organization entered the program.

Financing Religion with State Funds

Financial backing for the program reportedly came largely from Colson's Prison Fellowship Ministries, a not-for-profit organization that provided "funding to cover the salaries and benefits of program staff, the costs of Bible-based instructional and educational materials, and staff and volunteer training, materials and expenses." The Texas Department of Criminal Justice covered "security and day-to-day operating costs of the Vance Unit, including inmate support costs such as food, medical services and clothing."

Impressed by the apparent number of successful "graduates" who were released into the community and didn't recidivate, in 2001 the Seventy-seventh Texas Legislature, without a request from Colson, appropriated $1.5 million to expand the program. That not a single penny of this money was actually used can probably be attributed to Article 1, Section 7, of the Texas Constitution concerning Appropriations for Sectarian Purposes, which states: "No money shall be appropriated or drawn from the Treasury for the benefit of any sect, or religious society, theological or religious seminary; nor shall property belonging to the State be appropriated for any such purposes." In 2003 the Seventy-eighth Texas Legislature was obliged to make deep cuts in the state's budget and the $1.5 million was deleted.

Christianity to Heal Criminal Behavior

Critics correctly note that participants in Colson's program aren't given the option to refuse to profess a commitment to an agenda that is inherently religious. The website of Colson's organization explicitly states that the entire menu of social services touted as "non-sectarian" activities crucial for successful reintegration are offered to inmates "willing to participate in a Christ-centered biblically-based program." This is equivalent to a coerced nonchoice between salvation and damnation and hypocrisy by some inmates who perceive it as a one-way ticket to early release and freedom.

The theological doctrine of paramount importance to Colson—and certainly to all evangelical Christian groups with similar programs—is that criminal conduct is a manifestation of a person's sinful nature and the only cure comes from the miraculous power of God's grace and love. The guts of this widely shared belief is that all secular programs designed to rehabilitate in a therapeutic model of creating and restoring human relationships are doomed to failure. This belief is embraced by Bush and is the key to understanding his belief in the near total ineptitude of governmental policies and programs created to improve the lives of citizens.

The Creation of Faith-Based Prisons

The spread of faith-based prisons is due primarily to the influence of Bush and his ideological twin brother, Jeb (governor of Florida). In 2003 Jeb Bush proudly dedicated the first faith-based prison in the United States: a 750-bed medium security facility for males in Lawtey, Florida. Like his brother in the White House, he claims that the only way to achieve real rehabilitation of criminals and reduce recidivism is to "lead them to God." Florida advocates of this program claim that the prison consists entirely of 700 to 750 male inmates with a professed desire to be rehabilitated who are being voluntarily led to achieve this goal by committing their lives to a god of their choosing through Islam, Judaism, or Christianity. In April 2004 Florida opened its second faith-based prison for more than 300 female inmates in the Hillsborough unit in Riverview.

The eligibility criteria for acceptance into both of these faith-based prisons contain an inherent programmatic contradiction that isn't mentioned, is dismissed as superfluous, or isn't perceived by its advocates. Participants aren't required to profess belief in any god, aren't required to attend any religious courses, but they must articulate a commitment to believing they can be changed. Admitting that a person can be a successful graduate without a belief in a god or attending any religious services deals a death-blow to any form of argument that morality is inseparably linked to religion and that a religious "conversion" is necessary to produce a permanent change in the thinking and conduct of any person.

Texas and Florida are the leading wagons in the train of faith-based programs for prison inmates. Other wagons include Georgia, Iowa, Tennessee, Minnesota, Kansas, Maryland, California, and Ohio. And, not surprisingly, Corrections Cor-

Court Ruling on Faith-Based Prison Rehabilitation Programs

In early 2003, Americans United for Separation of Church and State joined with a group of Iowa taxpayers and inmates to challenge the InnerChange program in federal court.

In ruling on that case, Judge [Robert W.] Pratt noted that the born-again Christian staff was the sole judge of an inmate's spiritual transformation. If an inmate did not join in the religious activities that were part of his "treatment," the staff could write up disciplinary reports, generating demerits the inmate's parole board might see. Or they could expel the inmate.

And while the program was supposedly open to all, in practice its content was "a substantial disincentive" for inmates of other faiths to join, the judge noted. Although the ministry itself does not condone hostility toward Catholics, Roman Catholic inmates heard their faith criticized by staff members and volunteers from local evangelical churches, the judge found. And Jews and Muslims in the program would have been required to participate in Christian worship services even if that deeply offended their own religious beliefs.

Diana B. Henriques and Andrew Lehren,
New York Times, *December 10, 2006.*

poration of America (CCA)—the United States' largest owner and operator of private prisons, based in Nashville, Tennessee, and motivated by the smell of fresh state and federal dollars—has joined forces with the Chicago-based Institute in Basic Life Principles, a Christian evangelical organization committed to the view that only Jesus Christ, the son of God, can change lives.

Bill Berkowitz [critic of the conservative movement], in his September 4, 2004, WorkingForChange column, "Prisons, Profits, and Prophets," writes that the short-term goal of this partnership is to enroll up to 1,000 inmates in CCA prisons. Earlier in April 2003 the CCA entered into a "full-scale partnership" with a Dallas-based evangelical Christian group called Champions for Life. The goal of that alignment was to, within three years, have in place "religious-oriented prison programs" in all of CCA's sixty-four facilities, containing more than 60,000 inmates. But these partnerships are nothing but sick jokes. The CCA has been plagued by a history of lawsuits, including accusations of prisoner abuse, and is accountable only to stockholders, not the public interest.

Historical Origins

Historically considered, the first faith-based programs for prison inmates were in Louisiana. In 1995 the New Orleans Baptist Theological Seminary officially launched a course of studies culminating in undergraduate degrees for inmates in the infamous prison in Angola, Louisiana. The credit for initiating this program belongs to Burl Cain, a devout Southern Baptist and the warden of the Angola prison. The story of Cain's campaign to spiritually transform one of the nation's toughest prisons from which very few prisoners will ever leave is a powerful and persuasive argument for prison inmates to engage in religious studies. Supposedly, the seminary and private donations cover the majority of expenses for this biblically oriented program, which, according to Cain, has made Angola "more peaceful than New Orleans," so "God reigns at Angola." The fact remains, however, as acknowledged by Cain, that a significant number of tax dollars are used to support this Southern Baptist version of evangelical Christianity.

Hypocrisy of the Administration

The combined efforts of these religious groups can be credited with leading a relatively large number of inmates to life-

changing transformations and productive lives. Anyone, therefore, who voices opposition to the distribution of state and
federal revenue to religious organizations providing spiritual
guidance capable of transforming the lives of thousands of
hardened criminals is going to be portrayed as an opponent
of motherhood and apple pie. And the totally pragmatic justification of programs that achieve positive results is persuasive.

But the president emphatically denies it is the responsibility of the government to provide all inmates in our nations'
prisons the same kind of social services that are essential components of all effective faith-based programs. On February 10,
2003, in a speech at the Opryland Hotel in Nashville, Tennessee, promoting his faith-based initiative, George W. Bush declared:

> We've arrested and we convict criminals; yet building more
> prisons will not substitute for responsibility and order in
> our souls. The role of government is limited because gov-
> ernment cannot put hope in people's hearts or a sense of
> purpose in people's lives. That happens when someone puts
> an arm around a neighbor and says, "God loves you, I love
> you, and you can count on us both."

These comments are a loud and clear commitment to the
beliefs that governmental policies and programs can't and
shouldn't attempt to promote virtuous conduct in the lives of
citizens.

In response to anyone who criticizes his religious crusade
with the suggestion that he is blurring, if not potentially de-
stroying, church-state separation, the president replies in a
cavalier style and invokes a totally specious distinction in support of his position. In an interview with *Christianity Today*,
during which the paramount issue of church-state separation
was raised, Bush confidently stated:

> We're funding people and programs, not institutions. Some
> of my opponents worry about proselytization. I believe the

power of the church is the capacity to change the heart, and we should not force the church to change its mission.

The entire "faith-based initiative" of the Bush administration is mired in a constitutional minefield with numerous lawsuits filed by organizations alleging the violation of church-state separation. Some prominent religious leaders are claiming that the government is using all religions in this country as a dumping ground for the nation's social ills. The government, they say, has abandoned its responsibility by using the scent-laden lures of state and federal grants for nonprofit charitable organizations to create and provide a myriad of social services. The irony of this situation is the frequently heard complaint that bureaucratic red tape designed to protect the line between church and state is preventing religious organizations from fulfilling their mission. And it is certainly important to note that some religious leaders of the Protestant, Catholic, and Jewish faiths have gone on record with statements that the president's entire faith-based action plan violates the separation of church and state.

Questionable Claims of Success

Most, if not all organizations with faith-based programs for prison inmates release reports claiming to scientifically demonstrate a high success rate of participants and a significant reduction of recidivism. Again, while not doubting that many lives are permanently redirected in a positive direction, the temptation to "cook the books" to achieve the desired results and engage in "casuistry" [case-based reasoning] is too strong for some to resist. Colson's Prison Fellowship Ministries is probably the most prominent example of resorting to what Mark A.R. Kleiman characterizes as:

> one of the oldest tricks on the books, one almost guaranteed to make a success of any program: counting the win-

ners and ignoring the losers. The technical form for this in statistics is "selection bias"; program managers know it as "creaming."

In his August 5, 2003, *Slate* article, "Faith-Based Fudging," Kleiman comments on 75 of 177 volunteer inmates who graduated from Colson's program at the Vance prison unit in Texas:

Graduation involved sticking with the program, not only in prison but after release. No one counted as a graduate, for example, unless he got a job. Naturally, the graduates did better than the control group. Anything that selects out from a group of ex-inmates who hold jobs is going to look like a miracle cure, because getting a job is among the very best predictors of staying out of trouble. And inmates who stick with a demanding program of self-improvement through 16 months probably have more inner resources, and a stronger determination to turn their lives around, than the average inmate.

The InnerChange [religion-based rehabilitation program for Iowa prisoners] cheerleaders simply ignored the other 102 participants who dropped out, were kicked out, or got early parole and didn't finish. Naturally, the non-graduates did worse than the control group. If you select out the winners, you leave mostly losers.

Kleiman's final judgment is that "probably no one was actually lying; they were just believing, and repeating as a fact, what they wanted to believe." But perhaps Colson's loyal troops, like the Catholic Jesuits in the seventeenth century, used some complex reasoning (casuistry) to justify moral laxity.

Another flagrant example of this kind of reasoning is found in the earlier cited evaluation report on Colson's program written by the staff of the Texas Criminal Justice Policy Council and approved by its director, Tony Fabelo. In his

"Note from the Director," Fabelo claims that, because the $1.5 million appropriated by the Texas legislature for the expansion of this program wasn't used, it

> has operated at no cost to the taxpayer.... Even if early outcome results in terms of reduction in recidivism are not dramatically better than some programs operated by the state, improvements in the Inner Freedom Initiative program may result in better outcomes in the future and those outcomes will have been achieved at no cost to the taxpayer.

Unfair and Unconstitutional

Collectively considered, all of the states with faith-based programs for prison inmates are spending millions of tax dollars in direct or indirect payment for religious-oriented programs to salvage the lives of a select few while doing little to change the lives of the vast majority of inmates—most of whom will eventually be released with or without some form of supervision. The remedy for this blatantly unfair and unconstitutional expenditure of state revenue is, first, to abolish it and, second, to develop a new and more inclusive agenda for changing lives and reducing recidivism.

I have no reason to doubt or criticize the fact that President George W. Bush is a born-again Christian whose less than exemplary life was transformed by his conversion to some religious beliefs. Although I don't agree with those who argue that he is a malicious bigot and hypocrite cloaked in the guise of a compassionate evangelical Christian, I am unconditionally persuaded that he is sincerely and profoundly wrong in his advocacy of the "faith-based agenda" spawned during his tenure as governor of Texas. I believe that his presidential plan to cure the nation's social ills through the ministries of religious organizations is an insidious threat to the constitutional separation of church and state. All faith-based programs for prison inmates to which state revenue is distributed either directly or indirectly through sectarian religious organizations are an egregious constitutional violation.

Periodical Bibliography

The following articles have been selected to supplement the diverse views presented in this chapter.

Scott D. Camp — "An Exploration into Participation in a Faith-Based Prison Program," *Criminology & Public Policy*, August 2006.

Jim Dwyer — "Less Crime: No Reason to Shut Prisons," *New York Times*, April 12, 2008.

Carol Fennelly — "Who Does the Time?" *Sojourners*, September–October 2007.

Marie Gottschalk — "Dollars, Sense, and Penal Reform: Social Movements and the Future of the Carceral State," *Social Research*, Summer 2007.

Harriet Hall — "Hope for Reentering the Community," *Behavioral Healthcare*, March 2008.

Glenn C. Loury — "America Incarcerated," *Utne Reader*, November–December 2007.

Marc Mauer — "The Hidden Problem of Time Served in Prison," *Social Research*, Summer 2007.

Donald Nadler — "Calculating the Cost of Inmates in Jail," *American Jails*, March–April 2008.

Jacob Sullum — "Incarceration Nation," *Reason*, June 2008.

Jeremy Travis — "Reflections on the Reentry Movement," *Federal Sentencing Reporter*, December 2007.

OPPOSING
VIEWPOINTS®
SERIES

Should Sentencing Laws Be Reformed?

Chapter Preface

In 2006, the United States Supreme Court declined to hear the case of Weldon Angelos, a twenty-six-year-old aspiring hip hop mogul and resident of Salt Lake City, Utah, who had been sentenced to fifty-five years in prison in 2003 for charges of possession of a weapon during the commission of a felony. Angelos had been indicted on multiple marijuana distribution charges after selling $350 worth of marijuana to a police informant on three separate occasions. Angelos was carrying a pistol strapped to his leg at the time of two of the transactions, but he did not display the weapon. During the other deal, the gun was supposedly in his car. A search of his home a year later turned up three guns and $19,000.

Angelos, who had no prior criminal record, was offered a plea bargain of fifteen years, but he turned down the deal. Upon his refusal, three counts for carrying a weapon were added to Angelos' drug charges—a bonus made possible by the federal mandatory minimum sentencing statute that penalizes drug dealers for weapons possession. The first count added five years to Angelos' sentence and each additional count called for a mandatory twenty-five year addition to his sentence.

In the majority of cases these weapon charges are not included in prosecuting drug offenders. According to a statement released by the United States Sentencing Commission in 2000, only 10 to 30 percent of drug offenders who used or carried a gun received extended sentences because many prosecutors do not push for the mandatory sentencing. In Angelo's case, however, his refusal to plea bargain made him seem impudent to federal prosecutors in Salt Lake City, and they made the decision to pursue the harshest penalty.

The presiding judge in Angelos' case, Paul Cassell, resisted sentencing a nonviolent first-time offender to the mandatory minimum sentence, and first chose to obtain the opinions of the jurors in deciding Angelos' sentence. The jurors recommended an average sentence of 18 years. Judge Cassell then compared the sentences given for various violent crimes from terrorism to airplane hijacking, all of which earned convicts average sentences of less than 25 years. He asked President George W. Bush to show clemency in this case, but Cassell's complaints were ignored, and ultimately he had to follow the law. He wrote, "The court believes that to sentence Mr. Angelos to prison for the rest of his life is unjust, cruel, and even irrational. The court reluctantly concludes that it has no choice." He sentenced Weldon Angelos to fifty-five years and a day in prison.

In 2005 Angelos tried to have his sentence reexamined in a U.S. circuit court of appeals. On June 22 of that year, several judges and four former U.S. attorneys general wrote a brief to the circuit court to urge leniency. The pleas went unheeded, and Angelos' sentence remained. The day before the filing of the brief, then-U.S. Attorney General Alberto Gonzales spoke in support of mandatory minimum sentences, claiming there was a nationwide tendency among judges to use their discretion at sentencing and thus create a haphazard sentencing structure, which did not punish similar crimes equitably. The following chapter features these words of Gonzales's, as well as other viewpoints on issues surrounding the reformation of sentencing laws in America.

"Federal sentencing guidelines have helped keep Americans safe while also delivering on their promise to reduce unwarranted disparities in sentences."

Mandatory Minimum Sentences Are Necessary and Just

Alberto Gonzales

In the following viewpoint, Alberto Gonzales argues that mandatory federal sentencing guidelines are essential for ensuring both the safety of the American people and fairness within the criminal justice system. Gonzales voices concern with the Supreme Court decision of United States v. Booker, *which gives judges the ability to sentence outside of the guidelines mandated by the federal government. He believes that without mandatory guidelines, there will be increased disparity in sentences for different defendants who have committed similar crimes, as well as a drift toward lighter sentences. Alberto Gonzales was appointed to the position of Attorney General of the United States in May 2005 by President George W. Bush and resigned in September 2007.*

Alberto Gonzales, "Prepared Remarks of Attorney General Alberto Gonzales, Sentencing Guidelines Speech," June 21, 2005. www.usdoj.gov.

As you read, consider the following questions:

1. According to Gonzales's examples, how do the sentences given to two individuals who were charged with possession of child pornography differ?

2. What does Gonzales state to be the two goals of the Sentencing Reform Act of 1984?

3. What percentage of federal judges adhered to the sentencing guidelines in 2005 according the Sentencing Commission?

For decades, victims of crime lived in fear and suffered in silence. So-called experts told us that high levels of crime were inevitable, especially among the poor. The message to victims of crime—who were disproportionately poor as well—was inescapable: learn to live with it.

But thanks to the work of victims' groups and other concerned Americans, the status of victims of crime in America began to change. Victims, and their friends and loved ones, began to demand more from our system of justice.

Important policies designed to ensure the vindication of victims' rights in federal criminal cases have been developed during the [George W.] Bush Administration. [In 2004], the President signed the Justice For All Act [which protects the rights of crime victims]. I recently revised and reissued the Attorney General Guidelines For Victim and Witness Assistance [which outline the role of the U.S. Department of Justice in aiding victims of crime].

For victims, another key aspect of any fair and equitable criminal justice system is to ensure that those convicted of crimes serve tough and fair sentences. And since 1987, we have had a sentencing system for federal offenses that responded to this demand—and has helped to achieve the lowest crime rates in a generation.

The Negative Impact of *U.S. v. Booker*

The key to this system was a set of mandatory sentencing guidelines that specified a range within which federal judges were bound to impose sentences, absent unusual circumstances. The guidelines reflected a careful balancing by Congress and the Sentencing Commission [an independent agency in the judicial branch of the federal government responsible for establishing guidelines for federal courts] between discretion and consistency in sentencing. But the mandatory guidelines system is no longer in place today, and I believe its loss threatens the progress we have made in ensuring tough and fair sentences for federal offenders.

That threat is illustrated by the story of two defendants, both convicted of similar charges involving possession of child pornography, one in New York, the other across the Hudson River in New Jersey.

The New York defendant faced a sentencing range of 27 to 33 months in prison, but received only probation.

The New Jersey defendant faced a sentencing range of 30 to 37 months and was given a sentence of 41 months in prison.

What made the difference?

[In] January [2005], the Supreme Court ruled that federal sentencing guidelines mandated by bipartisan congressional majorities in 1984 are advisory only and are no longer binding on federal judges. In that case, *U.S. v. Booker*, the Court held that federal sentencing guidelines violated a defendant's rights under the Sixth Amendment of our Constitution. The result is that, today, judges must take the guidelines into account when sentencing, but are no longer bound by the law to impose a sentence within the range prescribed by the guidelines.

So in the New Jersey child pornography case, the judge deemed it necessary to protect the public from the defendant and imposed a sentence slightly above the guideline range. In the New York case, however, the judge reasoned that the defendant would benefit from continued psychological treatment and ordered probation only.

The story of these two defendants is just one example that illustrates a developing trend in the aftermath of the *Booker* decision. More and more frequently, judges are exercising their discretion to impose sentences that depart from the carefully considered ranges developed by the U.S. Sentencing Commission. In the process, we risk losing a sentencing system that requires serious sentences for serious offenders and helps prevent disparate sentences for equally serious crimes. . . .

Increasing Safety and Fairness

The federal sentencing guidelines were the result of Republicans and Democrats coming together in response to the high crime rates of the 1960s and 1970s to create an invaluable tool of justice. As the rates of serious violent felonies more than tripled, a consensus emerged that society needed to be protected from the early release of offenders.

Also undermining Americans' faith in the system was the fact that significant disparities existed in the sentences received by individuals guilty of equally serious offenses. A widespread and bipartisan consensus took hold that our system of sentencing was unfair and broken.

So in 1984, lawmakers from across the political spectrum passed the Sentencing Reform Act with two broad goals in mind. The first was to increase the safety of law-abiding Americans by restoring in sentencing an emphasis on punishment, incapacitation, and deterrence. The second was to ensure fairness in sentencing. The statute's guiding principle was consistency—defendants who had committed equally serious crimes and had similar criminal backgrounds should receive similar sentences, irrespective of their race or the race of their victim and irrespective of geographic location or economic background.

In the 17-plus years that they have been in existence, federal sentencing guidelines have achieved the ambitious goals of public safety and fairness set out by Congress. The United States is today experiencing crime rates that are the lowest in a generation. If crime rates during the last 10 years had been as high as the rates 30–40 years ago, then 34 million additional violent crimes would have been committed in the last decade.

Of course, no single law or policy is by itself responsible for today's low levels of violent crime. But multiple, independent studies of our criminal justice system confirm what our common sense tells us: increased incarceration means reduced crime, and federal and state sentencing reform has helped put the most violent, repeat offenders behind bars, and kept them there for sentences appropriate to their crimes.

Federal sentencing guidelines have helped keep Americans safe while also delivering on their promise to reduce unwarranted disparities in sentences. When the U.S. Sentencing Commission recently took stock of 15 years experience with the federal sentencing guidelines, it noted that studies by both the Commission itself and others have determined that the guidelines . . . "have succeeded at the job they were principally designed to do: reduce unwarranted disparity arising from differences among judges."

For 17 years, mandatory federal sentencing guidelines have helped drive down crime. The guidelines have evolved over time to adapt to changing circumstances and a better understanding of societal problems and the criminal justice system. Judges, legislators, the Sentencing Commission, prosecutors, defense lawyers, and others have worked hard to develop a system of sentencing guidelines that has protected Americans and improved American justice.

The Risks of an Advisory Guidelines System

I am concerned, however, that, under an advisory guidelines system, we will not be able to sustain this progress and victims may be victimized once again by a system that is intended to protect them.

And not because judges aren't doing their best in each and every case. Deciding the fate of a defendant is a serious and difficult task, and our judges discharge this obligation conscientiously and with integrity. As a former judge, I know well the difficulties of the task and I admire the men and women on our federal bench. But it is inevitable over time that, with so many different individual judges involved, exercising their own individual discretion, in so many different jurisdictions, shorter sentences and disparities among sentences will occur under a system of advisory guidelines.

And, indeed, the evidence the Department has seen since the *Booker* decision suggests an increasing disparity in sentences, and a drift toward lesser sentences.

Moreover, our U.S. Attorneys consistently report that a critical law enforcement tool has been taken from them. Under the sentencing guidelines, defendants were only eligible to receive reductions in sentences in exchange for cooperation when the government petitioned the court. Under the advisory guidelines system, judges are free to reduce sentences when they believe the defendant has sufficiently cooperated. And since defendants no longer face penalties that are serious and certain, key witnesses are increasingly less inclined to cooperate with prosecutors. We risk a return to the pre-guidelines era, when defendants were encouraged to "play the odds" in our criminal justice system, betting that the luck of the draw—the judge randomly assigned to their case—might result in a lighter sentence.

In one recent case, a South Carolina man pled guilty to federal weapons and drug trafficking charges. The firearms in his possession included a fully automatic machine gun, two assault rifles, and two pistols. After his arrest on these charges, this defendant was released on bond. While out on bond, he failed a drug test and absconded from electronic monitoring. Federal marshals caught up with him and, after a six-hour standoff, tear-gassed him out of the house where he was hid-

Mandatory Minimum Sentencing as a Tool for Prosecutors

In a way sentencing guidelines cannot, mandatory minimum statutes provide a level of uniformity and predictability in sentencing. . . . Equally important, mandatory minimum sentences provide an indispensable tool for prosecutors, because they provide the strongest incentive to defendants to cooperate against the others who were involved in their criminal activity.

In drug cases, where the ultimate goal is to rid society of the entire trafficking enterprise, mandatory minimum statutes are especially significant. Unlike a bank robbery, for which a bank teller or an ordinary citizen could be a critical witness, often in drug cases the critical witnesses are drug users and/or other drug traffickers. The offer of relief from a mandatory minimum sentence in exchange for truthful testimony allows the Government to move steadily and effectively up the chain of supply, using the lesser distributors to prosecute the more serious dealers and their leaders and suppliers. Mandatory minimum sentences are needed in appropriate circumstances, such as trafficking involving minors and trafficking in and around drug treatment centers.

Jodi L. Avergun, statement before the House Judiciary Committee Subcommittee on Crime, Terrorism, and Homeland Security, April 12, 2005.

ing. Under the federal sentencing guidelines, this individual, who had a long history of state charges related to assault and drug possession, faced up to 27 years in prison. However, post-*Booker*, the judge sentenced him to only 10, offering no explanation. The Department is appealing this unreasonably low sentence.

In other cases, defendants are receiving sentences dramatically lower than the guidelines range without any explanation, or on the basis of factors that could not be considered under the guidelines.

In a case involving white collar crime, a Kansas rancher got 1.8 million dollars in cattle loans, falsely claiming that he was using the money to buy live cattle. He even took bank officials to livestock pens and claimed that the cows he was showing them were purchased with loan proceeds, when, in fact he lost all the money speculating on the cattle futures market. He pled guilty to defrauding the bank and faced a sentencing range of 37 to 46 months under the guidelines. But the judge gave him probation only, reasoning, in part, that the defendant had suffered enough when the bank foreclosed on his house.

We have also seen how a system without mandatory guidelines led to a radically reduced sentence for a previously convicted felon convicted of evading federal taxes. This New York defendant was sentenced in 2003 for evading the payment of more than six million dollars in taxes by such means as moving out of the country valuable assets—including a fleet of Rolls Royces. Under the then-mandatory sentencing guidelines, the defendant was sentenced to 41 months in prison. The judge said he would have liked to impose a considerably lesser sentence, but felt constrained by the guidelines. A year and half later, after the *Booker* decision, the defendant petitioned the court for re-sentencing and the judge reduced his sentence to seven months in prison and seven months of home confinement. The judge noted that the defendant's age and the need to take care of his wife—not normally relevant sentencing factors pre-*Booker*—now justified a lesser sentence.

Sentencing Reform Is Imperative

The trend suggested by these examples is consistent with the statistics being compiled by the U.S. Sentencing Commission.

According to the Commission, sentencing within the guidelines by federal judges has fallen from almost 70 percent in 2003 to under 63 percent [in 2005]. This trend is troubling to me and should be troubling to all victims of crime.

After reviewing the data, consulting with our prosecutors in the field, and reaching out to other interested parties, I have come to the conclusion that the advisory guidelines system we currently have can and must be improved.

I know our judges are trying to do the right thing. They are acting in good faith as they perform one of the toughest—and most important—jobs in our society with great skill and integrity. But the goals of public safety and fairness sought by Congress in the Sentencing Reform Act are the expressed will of the American people. Our sentencing system works best when judges have some discretion, but discretion that is bounded by mandatory sentencing guidelines created through the legislative process.

Since the *Booker* decision, numerous legislative proposals have been suggested in response and they should all be studied and discussed. One that I believe would preserve the protections and principles of the Sentencing Reform Act, and is thus deserving of serious consideration, is the construction of a minimum guideline system.

Under such a system, the sentencing court would be bound by the guidelines minimum, just as it was before the *Booker* decision. The guidelines maximum, however, would remain advisory, and the court would be bound to consider it, but not bound to adhere to it, just as it is today under *Booker*.

Under this proposal, advisory maximum sentences would continue to give the courts the benefit of guidelines that reflect decades of wisdom and experience.

The advantages of a minimum guideline system are many. It would preserve the traditional division of responsibility between judges and juries in criminal cases and retain the important function of the U.S. Sentencing Commission in providing guidelines to the courts regarding sentencing. It would also allow judges some flexibility for extraordinary cases. And a minimum guideline system would be fully consistent with the Sixth Amendment, as interpreted by the Supreme Court.

I have an open mind about how to best restore fairness and consistency in sentencing and I look forward to hearing the views of other interested parties about the best way ahead. As we go forward, I believe we should be guided by a fundamental fact: sentencing reform has been a success in both reducing crime and reducing unwarranted disparities. It has made Americans safer and our system of justice fairer. For the past two decades there has been an ongoing, healthy debate over the specifics of the sentencing guidelines. But there has also been a bipartisan consensus in support of the principles of sentencing reform. Today, I pledge the resources of the Department of Justice to work with the Congress, the Judiciary, the Sentencing Commission, and other organizations—like the National Center for Victims of Crime—to design a sentencing system that responds to the needs and concerns of all those who share our commitment to providing protection to the American people and equal justice to defendants.

> *"Mandatory minimum laws take sentencing discretion away from judges, and dictate how many years a convicted drug offender will spend in prison."*

Mandatory Minimum Sentences Are Unnecessary and Unjust

Susan Helen Moran

Susan Helen Moran is a contributing writer for United Press International. In the following viewpoint, she presents the argument that mandatory minimum sentences lessen the role of the judge, and increase that of the state and federal prosecutors. The viewpoint contends that the alternative to inequitable mandatory sentencing is drug-treatment programs for the average drug offender.

As you read, consider the following questions:

1. Since the enactment of mandatory minimum sentencing for drug users, how much has the Federal Bureau of Prisons' budget increased?

2. Who is John P. Walters?

3. Why do some policy analysts say the crux of the matter is constitutional?

Several states are rolling back their mandatory minimum prison sentences for low-level drug offenders, according to a new report published by a Michigan think tank. Runaway prison costs, increases in drug purity and street availability, and tragic personal accounts of low-level drug offenders serving long prison sentences have convinced state lawmakers that the mandatory sentencing structures just don't work, the report says.

Analysts at several think tanks agree, but key Federal lawmakers and executives continue to support mandatory minimums, and plan to uphold them as the centerpiece of their 2002 federal drug policy agenda.

[In 2001], Louisiana, Connecticut, Indiana, Iowa, Mississippi, California, and North Dakota rolled back mandatory drug sentences, according to the report, "Let the Punishment Fit the Crime: Re-Thinking Mandatory Minimums," published by the Mackinac Center for Public Policy in Mackinac, Mich., Massachusetts, New York, Alabama, Georgia, New Mexico and Idaho are all considering revising their drug laws, the study says.

Mandatory Minimums Dictate Sentencing and Increase Inmate Numbers

Mandatory minimum laws take sentencing discretion away from judges, and dictate how many years a convicted drug offender will spend in prison. The sentences are based on the weight of drugs involved, but the evidence for the suspect's drug possession can be based solely on testimony by other drug dealers, who often receive reduced sentences for testifying. Opponents of these controversial laws say they give the sentencing power to state and federal prosecutors—many of whom have lengthened offenders' prison sentences by charging them with crimes that trigger mandatory terms, and by provisions such as consecutive sentencing.

"Legislators intended to target 'drug kingpins' and to deter drug use when they enacted mandatory sentencing laws," write the report's authors, Lawrence Reed, president of Mackinac, and Laura Sager, executive director of Families Against Mandatory Minimums [FAMM] in Washington. "But, the laws backfired. States are filling their prisons with low-level, often first-time offenders, while the kingpins at the top of the drug trade exchange information and assets [with law enforcement agencies] for lighter sentences."

"There is a near consensus today that arrests of street-level drug dealers have had little effect upon the price or availability of heroin or cocaine," said Eric Sterling, president of the Criminal Justice Policy Foundation in Washington in a recent speech given at the Center on National Policy. In addition, the average drug dealer holds a low-wage job and sells drugs part-time to obtain drugs for his or her own use, according to Sterling. Also, the time a dealer spends in prison does not affect recidivism rates, according to the Justice Department.

Despite this apparent ineffectiveness, mandatory sentences have greatly benefited the prison system, which has had to expand dramatically to accommodate all the new inmates created by these laws. Since the enactment of mandatory minimum sentencing for drug users, the budget of the Federal Bureau of Prisons increased by more than 1,350 percent, from $220 million in 1986 to $3 billion in 1997, according to a bill in the House of Representatives. The bill proposes to alter the Controlled Substances Act, part of the Federal criminal code, by replacing phrases such as "not less than 5 years," and "not less than 20 years" with the phrase "for any term of years."

Instead of Being Sentenced, Drug Offenders Should Be Treated

As early as the winter of 1999, evidence suggested that mandatory minimums did not have a significant impact on crime and arrest rates, according to a study released by the Sentencing and Corrections Center at the RAND Corp., titled "The Impact of Truth-in-Sentencing and Three Strikes Legislation."

"Mandatory minimum sentences . . . are a terrible mistake, a bipartisan one," said Joseph diGenova at a recent Cato Institute forum. DiGenova is a member of the legal policy advisory board at the Washington Legal Foundation, a think tank and public interest law firm in Washington.

"We should repeal Draconian sentences [and] have more diversion from the criminal justice system to drug treatment programs," said Sally Satel, at the forum. Satel is a fellow at the American Enterprise Institute.

Instead of criminal litigation, diGenova, a former U.S. Attorney during the Reagan administration, recommends civil litigation of low-level drug offenses and civil commitment of convicted offenders to coerce treatment.

"We need more drug courts, where coerced abstinence is required," he said.

Many county prosecutors and law enforcement officials in Michigan are enthusiastically backing a movement for a statewide drug court and drug treatment, according to the Mackinac report. National and statewide polls also indicate that citizens overwhelmingly support cost-effective treatment and carefully supervised alternatives to incarceration for many low-level drug offenders, write Reed and Sager.

"That's not being soft—but being smart—on crime—and in these difficult economic times . . . taxpayers will thank their legislators for finding courage to do the right thing," they say.

Providing Justice for Inequitable Mandatory Sentences

In addition, some analysts recommend instituting a national clemency commission, enacted by Congress to review sentences and then make recommendations to the president. The commission could address inequities resulting from manda-

United States v. Booker Makes Sentencing Guidelines Advisory

On June 24, 2004, the Supreme Court decided *Blakely v. Washington*, invalidating a sentence imposed under the State of Washington's sentencing guideline system. The Supreme Court held that the Washington guidelines violated the right to trial by jury under the Sixth Amendment of the United States Constitution. Although the Court stated that it expressed no opinion on the federal sentencing guidelines, the decision had an immediate impact on the federal criminal justice system. Following *Blakely*, district and circuit courts voiced varying opinions on the implication of the decision for federal sentencing and no longer uniformly applied the sentencing guidelines.

On January 12, 2005, the Supreme Court decided *Booker*, applying *Blakely* to the federal guideline system and determining that the mandatory application of the federal sentencing guidelines violated the right to trial by jury under the Sixth Amendment. The Court remedied the Sixth Amendment violation by excising the provisions in the Sentencing Reform Act that made the federal sentencing guidelines mandatory, thereby converting the mandatory system that had existed for almost 20 years into an advisory one.

United States Sentencing Commission, Final Report on the Impact of United States v. Booker *on Federal Sentencing, March 2006.*

tory sentences and obtain lesser sentences or, in some cases, full pardons for low-level offenders.

At the end of the Clinton administration, Sager's FAMM organization succeeded in gaining early release for Dorthy Gaines, who served six years of her 19-year federal sentence for her role in a drug conspiracy. Nine other low-level offenders out of about 20 for whom FAMM requested presidential pardon received clemency, according to the organization. A national clemency commission would allow many more cases to be reviewed, giving many more low-level offenders now serving long mandatory sentences a change at early release.

Reed, Sager and other opponents of mandatory minimums, however, suffered a setback last week when the Senate confirmed President George W. Bush's appointment of John P. Walters as the new drug czar. Walters, president of the neoconservative Philanthropy Foundation in Washington, before becoming drug czar, staunchly supported mandatory minimum sentencing for drug offenders. In his new position, Walters, formerly deputy assistant to William Bennett at the Department of Education, could do much to stop and even reverse the national trend to abolish minimum sentencing, at least on the federal level—in federal court cases.

During Senate confirmation hearings, Democratic senators raised concerns that Walters, as head of the Office of National Drug Control Policy [ONDCP], would not adequately reflect the nation's growing consensus that more emphasis should be put on drug treatment programs rather than longer required prison time for low-level offenders.

Sen. Thomas Patrick Leahy, D-Vt., accused Walters of making statements that "fl[y] in the face of widespread dissatisfaction with mandatory minimum sentences among policymakers and federal judges. Indeed, Chief Justice William Rhenquist, and the Judicial Conferences composed of representatives from all 12 federal circuits, have called for the repeal of federal mandatory minimum sentences," said Leahy, chair of the Senate Judiciary Committee.

Walters answered the concern, saying that he would review the current mandatory minimum system.

"I do not believe [Walters] is the best person to undertake the task," Leahy said.

"Walters' controversial and often incendiary writings on drug-related issues have been red meat for the right-wing of the Republican Party," said Sen. Richard Durbin, D-Ill.

Sen. Orrin Hatch, R-Utah, however, countered by saying that Walters "has a long, documented history of supporting drug treatment as an integral component of a balanced national drug control policy. During Mr. Walters' tenure at ONDCP, treatment funding increased 74 percent. This compares with an increase over eight years for the Clinton administration of a mere 17 percent."

"The drug legalization camp exaggerates the rate at which defendants are jailed solely for simple possession," said Hatch. "This camp also wants us to view those who sell drugs as 'nonviolent offenders.' Mr. Walters, to his credit, has had the courage to publicly refute these misleading statistics and claims. . . . Those who sell drugs, whatever type and whatever quantity, are not, to this father and grandfather, 'nonviolent offenders.' Not when each pill, each joint, each line, and each needle can and often does destroy a young person's life."

"Nonviolent first offenders face mandatory federal prison terms for possession only if they have been arrested with crack cocaine, and then only when the quantities involved are those associated with retail, street-level drug dealing," wrote William Bennett in a recent letter to the Washington Post. "The crux of the matter [is], should street-level drug dealers go to prison?" Bennett, now co-director of Empower America in Washington.

Other policy analysts strongly disagree, saying the crux of the matter is constitutional.

"Harsh mandatory sentencing laws . . . remove sentencing discretion from judges and dramatically lengthen prison sentences," write Reed and Sager.

"The judicial sentencing process should be returned to the discretion of judges, whose job it is to evaluate each individual case and ensure that the fairness and interest of justice is served," says a statement from the Criminal Justice Policy Foundation.

"An execution cannot be used to condemn killing; it is killing."

The Death Penalty Should Be Abolished

Amnesty International

In the following viewpoint, Amnesty International argues that government use of the death penalty as a form of punishment violates human rights as defined by the United Nations' Universal Declaration of Human Rights, and that because of this, the death penalty should be abolished. Additional factors Amnesty examines to support its call for the abolition of the death penalty include the possibility of an innocent person being sentenced to death and the lack of evidence supporting the claim that the threat of death as punishment deters crime. Amnesty International is a global organization dedicated to ensuring the preservation of human rights worldwide.

As you read, consider the following questions:

1. What fraction of countries worldwide has abolished the death penalty, according to Amnesty International?

2. Why does Amnesty International believe the death penalty might encourage people to commit politically motivated crimes or acts of terror?

3. What does the "argument for retribution" boil down to, in Amnesty International's view?

The time has come to abolish the death penalty worldwide. The case for abolition becomes more compelling with each passing year. Everywhere experience shows that executions brutalize those involved in the process. Nowhere has it been shown that the death penalty has any special power to reduce crime or political violence. In country after country, it is used disproportionately against the poor or against racial or ethnic minorities. It is also used as a tool of political repression. It is imposed and inflicted arbitrarily. It is an irrevocable punishment, resulting inevitably in the execution of people innocent of any crime. It is a violation of fundamental human rights.

[Since the late 1990s] an average of at least three countries a year have abolished the death penalty, affirming respect for human life and dignity. Yet too many governments still believe that they can solve urgent social or political problems by executing a few or even hundreds of their prisoners. Too many citizens in too many countries are still unaware that the death penalty offers society not further protection but further brutalization. Abolition is gaining ground, but not fast enough.

The death penalty, carried out in the name of the nation's entire population, involves everyone. Everyone should be aware of what the death penalty is, how it is used, how it affects them, how it violates fundamental rights.

The death penalty is the premeditated and cold-blooded killing of a human being by the state. The state can exercise no greater power over a person than that of deliberately depriving him or her of life. At the heart of the case for abolition, therefore, is the question of whether the state has the right to do so.

A Human Rights Issue

When the world's nations came together [in 1945] to found the United Nations (UN), few reminders were needed of what could happen when a state believed that there was no limit to what it might do to a human being. The staggering extent of state brutality and terror during World War II and the consequences for people throughout the world were still unfolding in December 1948, when the UN General Assembly adopted without dissent the Universal Declaration of Human Rights.

The Universal Declaration is a pledge among nations to promote fundamental rights as the foundation of freedom, justice and peace. The rights it proclaims are inherent in every human being. They are not privileges that may be granted by governments for good behaviour and they may not be withdrawn for bad behaviour. Fundamental human rights limit what a state may do to a man, woman or child.

No matter what reason a government gives for executing prisoners and what method of execution is used, the death penalty cannot be separated from the issue of human rights. The movement for abolition cannot be separated from the movement for human rights.

The Universal Declaration recognizes each person's right to life and categorically states further that "No one shall be subjected to torture or to cruel, inhuman or degrading treatment or punishment". In Amnesty International's view the death penalty violates these rights.

Self-defence may be held to justify, in some cases, the taking of life by state officials: for example, when a country is locked in warfare (international or civil) or when law-enforcement officials must act immediately to save their own lives or those of others. Even in such situations the use of lethal force is surrounded by internationally accepted legal safeguards to inhibit abuse. This use of force is aimed at countering the immediate damage resulting from force used by others.

The death penalty, however, is not an act of self-defence against an immediate threat to life. It is the premeditated killing of a prisoner who could be dealt with equally well by less harsh means.

State Subsidized Torture

There can never be a justification for torture or for cruel, inhumane or degrading treatment or punishment. The cruelty of the death penalty is evident. Like torture, an execution constitutes an extreme physical and mental assault on a person already rendered helpless by government authorities.

If hanging a woman by her arms until she experiences excruciating pain is rightly condemned as torture, how does one describe hanging her by the neck until she is dead? If administering 100 volts of electricity to the most sensitive parts of a man's body evokes disgust, what is the appropriate reaction to the administration of 2,000 volts to his body in order to kill him? If a pistol held to the head or a chemical substance injected to cause protracted suffering are clearly instruments of torture, how should they be identified when used to kill by shooting or lethal injection? Does the use of legal process in these cruelties make their inhumanity justifiable?

The physical pain caused by the action of killing a human being cannot be quantified. Nor can the psychological suffering caused by fore-knowledge of death at the hands of the state. Whether a death sentence is carried out six minutes after a summary trial, six weeks after a mass trial or 16 years after lengthy legal proceedings, the person executed is subjected to uniquely cruel, inhuman and degrading treatment and punishment.

Internationally agreed laws and standards stipulate that the death penalty can only be used after a fair judicial process. When a state convicts prisoners without affording them a fair trial, it denies the right to due process and equality before the law. The irrevocable punishment of death removes not only the victim's right to seek redress for wrongful conviction, but also the judicial system's capacity to correct its errors.

Like killings which take place outside the law, the death penalty denies the value of human life. By violating the right to life, it removes the foundation for realization of all rights enshrined in the Universal Declaration of Human Rights.

As the Human Rights Committee set up under the [UN's] International Covenant on Civil and Political Rights has recognized, "The right to life ... is the supreme right from which no derogation is permitted even in time of public emergency which threatens the life of the nation ..." In a general comment on Article 6 of the Covenant issued in 1982, the Committee concluded that "all measures of abolition [of the death penalty] should be considered as progress in the enjoyment of the right to life within the meaning of Article 40".

Many governments have recognized that the death penalty cannot be reconciled with respect for human rights. The UN has declared itself in favour of abolition. Two-thirds of the countries in the world have now abolished the death penalty in law or practice. . . .

Amnesty International's statistics also show a significant overall decline in the number of reported executions in 2006. In 2006, 91% of all known executions took place in a small number of countries: China, Iran, Iraq, Pakistan, Sudan and the USA. Europe is almost a death penalty-free-zone—the main exception being Belarus; in Africa only six states carried out executions in 2006; in the Americas only the USA has carried out executions since 2003.

Justifying the Death Penalty

Unlike torture, "disappearances" and extrajudicial executions, most judicial executions are not carried out in secret or denied by government authorities. Executions are often announced in advance. In some countries they are carried out in public or before a group of invited observers.

No government publicly admits to torture or other grave violations of human rights, although privately some officials may seek to justify such abuses in the name of the "greater good". But retentionist governments, those that keep the death penalty, for the most part openly admit to using it: they do not so much deny its cruelty as attempt to justify its use; and the arguments they use publicly to justify the death penalty resemble those that are used in private to justify other, secret abuses.

The most common justification offered is that, terrible as it is, the death penalty is necessary: it may be necessary only temporarily, but, it is argued, only the death penalty can meet a particular need of society. And whatever that need may be it is claimed to be so great that it justifies the cruel punishment of death.

The particular needs claimed to be served by the death penalty differ from time to time and from society to society. In some countries the penalty is considered legitimate as a means of preventing or punishing the crime of murder. Elsewhere it may be deemed indispensable to stop drug-trafficking, acts of political terror, economic corruption or adultery. In yet other countries, it is used to eliminate those seen as posing a political threat to the authorities.

Once one state uses the death penalty for any reason, it becomes easier for other states to use it with an appearance of legitimacy for whatever reasons they may choose. If the death penalty can be justified for one offence, justifications that accord with the prevailing view of a society or its rulers will be found for it to be used for other offences. Whatever purpose is cited, the idea that a government can justify a punishment as cruel as death conflicts with the very concept of human rights. The significance of human rights is precisely that some means may never be used to protect society because their use violates the very values which make society worth protecting. When this essential distinction between appropriate and inappropriate means is set aside in the name of some "greater good", all rights are vulnerable and all individuals are threatened.

No Evidence for Deterrence

The death penalty, as a violation of fundamental human rights, would be wrong even if it could be shown that it uniquely met a vital social need. What makes the use of the death penalty even more indefensible and the case for its abolition even more compelling is that it has never been shown to have any special power to meet any genuine social need.

Countless men and women have been executed for the stated purpose of preventing crime, especially the crime of murder. Yet Amnesty International has failed to find convincing evidence that the death penalty has any unique capacity to deter others from commiting particular crimes. A survey of research findings on the relation between the death penalty and homicide rates, conducted for the UN in 1988 and updated in 2002, concluded: ". . . it is not prudent to accept the hypothesis that capital punishment deters murder to a marginally greater extent than does the threat and application of the supposedly lesser punishment of life imprisonment".

Undeniably the death penalty, by permanently "incapacitating" a prisoner, prevents that person from repeating the crime. But there is no way to be sure that the prisoner would indeed have repeated the crime if allowed to live, nor is there any need to violate the prisoner's right to life for the purpose of incapacitation: dangerous offenders can be kept safely away from the public without resorting to execution, as shown by the experience of many abolitionist countries.

Nor is there evidence that the threat of the death penalty will prevent politically motivated crimes or acts of terror. If anything, the possibility of political martyrdom through execution may encourage people to commit such crimes.

Death Penalty Executions by State

January 17, 1977 to June 4, 2007 (Total to date: 1,075*)

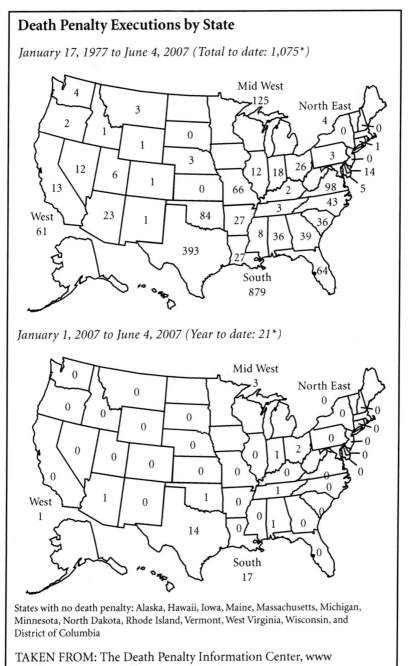

January 1, 2007 to June 4, 2007 (Year to date: 21*)

States with no death penalty: Alaska, Hawaii, Iowa, Maine, Massachusetts, Michigan, Minnesota, North Dakota, Rhode Island, Vermont, West Virginia, Wisconsin, and District of Columbia

TAKEN FROM: The Death Penalty Information Center, www .deathpenaltyinfo.org.

Every society seeks protection from crimes. Far from being a solution, the death penalty gives the erroneous impression that "firm measures" are being taken against crime. It diverts attention from the more complex measures which are really needed. In the words of the South African Constitution Court in 1995, "We would be deluding ourselves if we were to believe that the execution of . . . a comparatively few people each year . . . will provide the solution to the unacceptably high rate of crime . . . The greatest deterrent to crime is the likelihood that offenders will be apprehended, convicted and punished".

The Dangerous Logic of Retribution

When the arguments of deterrence and incapacitation fall away, one is left with a more deep-seated justification for the death penalty: that of just retribution for the particular crime committed. According to this argument, certain people deserve to be killed as repayment for the evil done: there are crimes so offensive that killing the offender is the only just response.

It is an emotionally powerful argument. It is also one which, if valid, would invalidate the basis for human rights. If a person who commits a terrible act can "deserve" the cruelty of death, why cannot others, for similar reasons, "deserve" to be tortured or imprisoned without trial or simply shot on sight? Central to fundamental human rights is that they are inalienable. They may not be taken away even if a person has committed the most atrocious of crimes. Human rights apply to the worst of us as well as to the best of us, which is why they protect all of us.

What the argument for retribution boils down to, is often no more than a desire for vengeance masked as a principle of justice. The desire for vengeance can be understood and acknowledged but the exercise of vengeance must be resisted.

The history of the endeavour to establish the rule of law is a history of the progressive restriction of personal vengeance in public policy and legal codes.

If today's penal systems do not sanction the burning of an arsonist's home, the rape of the rapist or the torture of the torturer, it is not because they tolerate the crimes. Instead, it is because societies understand that they must be built on a different set of values from those they condemn.

An execution cannot be used to condemn killing; it is killing. Such an act by the state is the mirror image of the criminal's willingness to use physical violence against a victim.

Innocent People Will Be Executed

Related to the argument that some people "deserve" to die is the proposition that the state is capable of determining exactly who they are. Whatever one's view of the retribution argument may be, the practice of the death penalty reveals that no criminal justice system is, or conceivably could be, capable of deciding fairly, consistently and infallibly who should live and who should die.

All criminal justice systems are vulnerable to discrimination and error. Expediency, discretionary decisions and prevailing public opinion may influence the proceedings at every stage from the initial arrest to the last-minute decision clemency. The reality of the death penalty is that what determines who shall be executed and who shall be spared is often not only the nature of the crimes but also the ethnic and social background, the financial means or the political opinions of the defendant. The death penalty is used disproportionately against the poor, the powerless, the marginalised or those whom repressive governments deem it expedient to eliminate.

Human uncertainty and arbitrary judgements are factors which affect all judicial decisions. But only one decision—the decision to execute—results in something that cannot be remedied or undone. Whether executions take place within hours of a summary trial or after years of protracted legal proceedings, states will continue to execute people who are later found to be innocent. Those executed cannot be compensated for loss of life and the whole society must share responsibility for what has been done.

Abolition Is the Only Answer

It is the irrevocable nature of the death penalty, the fact that the prisoner is eliminated forever, that makes the penalty so tempting to some states as a tool of repression. Thousands have been put to death under one government only to be recognized as innocent victims when another set of authorities comes to power. Only abolition can ensure that such political abuse of the death penalty will never occur.

When used to crush political dissent, the death penalty is abhorrent. When invoked as a way to protect society from crime, it is illusory. Wherever used, it brutalizes those involved in the process and conveys to the public a sense that killing a defenceless prisoner is somehow acceptable. It may be used to try to bolster the authority of the state—or of those who govern in its name. But any such authority it confers is spurious. The penalty is a symbol of terror and, to that extent, a confession of weakness. It is always a violation of the most fundamental human rights.

Each society and its citizens have the choice to decide about the sort of world people want and will work to achieve: a world in which the state is permitted to kill as a legal punishment or a world based on respect for human life and human rights—a world without executions.

| *"Capital punishment produces a strong deterrent effect that saves lives."*

The Death Penalty Should Not Be Abolished

David B. Muhlhausen

In the following viewpoint, David B. Muhlhausen argues that capital punishment should not be abandoned because it deters crimes, saves lives, and the majority of American citizens support its use. Additionally, he maintains that evidence does not support claims that racial discrimination results in a disproportionate number of African Americans incarcerated on death row. David B. Muhlhausen is a senior policy analyst in the area of criminal justice for the Heritage Foundation, a conservative public policy research organization.

As you read, consider the following questions:

1. According to the 2006 study conducted by the RAND Corporation, what affects whether the death penalty is sought as punishment for a crime?

2. What are the three findings of Joanna M. Shepherd's analysis of data from 1977 to 1999 on the death penalty?

David B. Muhlhausen, "The Death Penalty Deters Crime and Saves Lives," Heritage Foundation, August 28, 2007. www.heritage.org. Reproduced by permission of the author.

3. Based on research conducted by H. Naci Mocan and R. Kaj Gittings, how many murders result from each commutation of a death row sentence?

While opponents of capital punishment have been very vocal in their opposition, Gallup opinion polls consistently demonstrate that the American public overwhelmingly supports capital punishment. In Gallup's most recent poll, 67 percent of Americans favor the death penalty for those convicted of murder, while only 28 percent are opposed. From 2000 to the most recent poll in 2006, support for capital punishment consistently runs a 2:1 ratio in favor.

Despite strong public support for capital punishment, federal, state, and local officials must continually ensure that its implementation rigorously upholds constitutional protections, such as due process and equal protection of the law. However, the criminal process should not be abused to prevent the lawful imposition of the death penalty in appropriate capital cases.

Crime Characteristics More Important Than Race

As of December 2005, there were 37 prisoners under a sentence of death in the federal system. Of these prisoners, 43.2 percent were white, while 54.1 percent were African-American. The fact that African-Americans are a majority of federal prisoners on death row and a minority in the overall United States population may lead some to conclude that the federal system discriminates against African-Americans. However, there is little rigorous evidence that such disparities exist in the federal system.

Under a competitive grant process, the National Institute of Justice awarded the RAND Corporation a grant to determine whether racial disparities exist in the federal death penalty system. The resulting 2006 RAND study set out to determine what factors, including the defendant's race, victim's race, and crime characteristics, affect the decision to seek a death penalty case. Three independent teams of researchers were tasked with developing their own methodologies to analyze the data. Only after each team independently drew their own conclusions did they share their findings with each other.

When first looking at the raw data without controlling for case characteristics, RAND found that large race effects with the decision to seek the death penalty are more likely to occur when the defendants are white and when the victims are white. However, these disparities disappeared in each of the three studies when the heinousness of the crimes was taken into account. The RAND study concludes that the findings support the view that decisions to seek the death penalty are driven by characteristics of crimes rather than by race. RAND's findings are very compelling because three independent research teams, using the same data but different methodologies, reached the same conclusions.

While there is little evidence that the federal capital punishment system treats minorities unfairly, some may argue that the death penalty systems in certain states may be discriminatory. One such state is Maryland. In May 2001, then-Governor Parris Glendening instituted a moratorium on the use of capital punishment in Maryland in light of concerns that it may be unevenly applied to minorities, especially African-Americans. In 2000, Governor Glendening commissioned University of Maryland Professor of Criminology Ray Paternoster to study the possibility of racial discrimination in the application of the death penalty in Maryland. The results of Professor Paternoster's study found that black defendants who murder white victims are substantially more likely to be charged with a capital crime and sentenced to death.

In 2003, Governor Robert L. Ehrlich wisely lifted the moratorium. His decision was justified. In 2005, a careful review of the study by Professor of Statistics and Sociology Richard

Berk of the University of California, Los Angeles, and his co-authors found that the results of Professor Paternoster's study do not stand up to statistical scrutiny. According to Professor Berk's re-analysis, "For both capital charges and death sentences, race either played no role or a small role that is very difficult to specify. In short, it is very difficult to find convincing evidence for racial effects in the Maryland data and if there are any, they may not be additive." Further, race may have a small influence because "cases with a black defendant and white victim or 'other' racial combination are *less* likely to have a death sentence."

The Death Penalty Deters Crime

Federal, state, and local officials need to recognize that the death penalty saves lives. How capital punishment affects murder rates can be explained through general deterrence theory, which supposes that increasing the risk of apprehension and punishment for crime deters individuals from committing crime. Nobel laureate Gary S. Becker's seminal 1968 study of the economics of crime assumed that individuals respond to the costs and benefits of committing crime.

According to deterrence theory, criminals are no different from law-abiding people. Criminals [economist Paul H. Rubin writes] "rationally maximize their own self-interest (utility) subject to constraints (prices, incomes) that they face in the marketplace and elsewhere." Individuals make their decisions based on the net costs and benefits of each alternative. Thus, deterrence theory provides a basis for analyzing how capital punishment should influence murder rates. Over the years, several studies have demonstrated a link between executions and decreases in murder rates. In fact, studies done in recent years, using sophisticated panel data methods, consistently demonstrate a strong link between executions and reduced murder incidents.

The Moral Importance of the Death Penalty

Punishment has its origins in the demand for justice, and justice is demanded by angry, morally indignant men, men who are angry when someone else is robbed, raped, or murdered. . . . This anger is an expression of their caring, and the just society needs citizens who care for each other, and for the community of which they are parts. One of the purposes of punishment, particularly capital punishment, is to recognize the legitimacy of that righteous anger and to satisfy and thereby to reward it. In this way, the death penalty, when duly or deliberately imposed, serves to strengthen the moral sentiments required by a self-governing community.

Walter Berns, The Weekly Standard, *February 4, 2008.*

The rigorous examination of the deterrent effect of capital punishment began with research in the 1970s by Isaac Ehrlich, currently a University of Buffalo Distinguished Professor of Economics. Professor Ehrlich's research found that the death penalty had a strong deterrent effect. While his research was debated by other scholars, additional research by Professor Ehrlich reconfirmed his original findings. In addition, research by Professor Stephen K. Layson of the University of North Carolina at Greensboro strongly reconfirmed Ehrlich's previous findings.

The Death Penalty Saves Lives

Numerous studies published over the past few years, using panel data sets [statisticians make distinctions between panel sets vs. what they call "one-dimensional," or "cross-sectional" data sets] and sophisticated social science techniques, are demonstrating that the death penalty saves lives. Panel studies observe multiple units over several periods. The addition of multiple data collection points gives the results of capital punishment panel studies substantially more credibility than the results of studies that have only single before-and-after intervention measures. Further, the longitudinal nature of the panel data allows researchers to analyze the impact of the death penalty over time that cross-sectional data sets cannot address.

Using a panel data set of over 3,000 counties from 1977 to 1996, Professors Hashem Dezhbakhsh, Paul R. Rubin, and Joanna M. Shepherd of Emory University found that each execution, on average, results in 18 fewer murders. Using state-level panel data from 1960 to 2000, Professors Dezhbakhsh and Shepherd were able to compare the relationship between executions and murder incidents before, during, and after the U.S. Supreme Court's death penalty moratorium. They found that executions had a highly significant negative relationship with murder incidents. Additionally, the implementation of state moratoria is associated with the increased incidence of murders.

Separately, Professor Shepherd's analysis of monthly data from 1977 to 1999 found three important findings.

First, each execution, on average, is associated with three fewer murders. The deterred murders included both crimes of passion and murders by intimates.

Second, executions deter the murder of whites and African-Americans. Each execution prevents the murder of one white person, 1.5 African-Americans, and 0.5 persons of other races.

Third, shorter waits on death row are associated with increased deterrence. For each additional 2.75-year reduction in the death row wait until execution, one murder is deterred.

Commuting Death Penalty Sentences Is Deadly

Professors H. Naci Mocan and R. Kaj Gittings of the University of Colorado at Denver have published two studies confirming the deterrent effect of capital punishment. The first study used state-level data from 1977 to 1997 to analyze the influence of executions, commutations, and removals from death row on the incidence of murder. For each additional execution, on average, about five murders were deterred. Alternatively, for each additional commutation, on average, five additional murders resulted. A removal from death row by either state courts or the U.S. Supreme Court is associated with an increase of one additional murder. Addressing criticism of their work, Professors Mocan and Gittings conducted additional analyses and found that their original findings provided robust support for the deterrent effect of capital punishment.

Two studies by Paul R. Zimmerman, a Federal Communications Commission economist, also support the deterrent effect of capital punishment. Using state-level data from 1978 to 1997, Zimmerman found that each additional execution, on average, results in 14 fewer murders. Zimmerman's second study, using similar data, found that executions conducted by electrocution are the most effective at providing deterrence.

Using a small state-level data set from 1995 to 1999, Professor Robert B. Ekelund of Auburn University and his colleagues analyzed the effect that executions have on single incidents of murder and multiple incidents of murder. They found that executions reduced single murder rates, while there was no effect on multiple murder rates.

In summary, the recent studies using panel data techniques have confirmed what we learned decades ago: Capital punishment does, in fact, save lives. Each additional execution appears to deter between three and 18 murders. While opponents of capital punishment allege that it is unfairly used against African-Americans, each additional execution deters the murder of 1.5 African-Americans. Further moratoria, commuted sentences, and death row removals appear to increase the incidence of murder.

The strength of these findings has caused some legal scholars, originally opposed to the death penalty on moral grounds, to rethink their case. In particular, Professor Cass R. Sunstein of the University of Chicago has commented:

> If the recent evidence of deterrence is shown to be correct, then opponents of capital punishment will face an uphill struggle on moral grounds. If each execution is saving lives, the harms of capital punishment would have to be very great to justify its abolition, far greater than most critics have heretofore alleged.

Americans support capital punishment for two good reasons. First, there is little evidence to suggest that minorities are treated unfairly. Second, capital punishment produces a strong deterrent effect that saves lives.

| *"Keeping offenders in prison for a longer period of time does not necessarily contribute significantly to reducing recidivism."*

Crack Cocaine Sentencing Laws Should Be Reformed Retroactively

Marc Mauer

In the following viewpoint, Marc Mauer argues that mandatory minimum sentences for crack cocaine offenders should be amended retroactively, resulting in the release of many prisoners sentenced to unjustly long prison confinement due to outdated laws that increased the penalty for crack cocaine possession. He contends that releasing these inmates would pose little threat to public safety, would save the prison system money, and would correct the racial discrimination that was evident in crack cocaine sentencing during the 1980s. This viewpoint was taken from Mauer's testimony before the United States Sentencing Commission in November 2007. In December 2007, the commission voted to allow some federal inmates to seek retroactive sentence reductions for crack cocaine violations, but delayed imple-

Marc Mauer, "Testimony before the United States Sentencing Commission, Hearing on Retroactivity of the Crack Cocaine Guideline Amendment," The Sentencing Project, November 13, 2007, pp. 1–5. Reproduced by permission of the author.

mentation pending Congressional hearings. Marc Mauer is director of the Sentencing Project, an organization dedicated to ensuring a fair criminal justice system and promoting alternatives to incarceration.

As you read, consider the following questions:

1. In Mauer's opinion, what factors confirm that releasing crack cocaine offenders early will not have a negative effect on public safety?

2. According to Mauer, how many years in prison will many of the offenders, released in accordance with a retroactive amendment, have already served?

3. If 19,000 prisoners received 27 month reductions in their sentences, how much money does the author estimate could be saved over a period of 30 years?

I have been engaged on the issue of crack cocaine sentencing policy for many years. Within the past year, my organization [the Sentencing Project] has submitted comments and presented testimony to the [U.S. Sentencing] Commission in preparation for its 2007 report and guideline amendment. We have also submitted amicus briefs to the U.S. Supreme Court in the [*United States v.*] *Claiborne* and *Kimbrough* [*v. United States*] cases regarding sentencing for crack cocaine offenses. I am here today [November 13, 2007] to urge the Commission to make the guideline amendment retroactive.

We have previously submitted a letter to the Commission providing an analysis of why we believe the amendment should be made retroactive. That letter argues that doing so would be consistent with the mandate of the Commission and previous amendments that have been made retroactive. We contend that: the amendment has an important purpose; it would be significant for the prisoners who would be affected; retroactive application would not be administratively difficult; and, retroactivity would address longstanding problems of racial disparity. . . .

A Retroactive Amendment and Public Safety

As the Commission has documented, applying the amendment retroactively would reduce average sentences by 27 months, although nearly two-thirds (63.5%) of offenders would receive a reduction of 24 months or less. Because of this sentence reduction, a concern that the Commission may address in consideration of retroactivity is whether applying the amendment to current offenders will have consequences for public safety. In this regard, there is no reason to believe that doing so will cause any undue negative consequences that cannot be adequately addressed.

The absence of any significant negative effect on public safety stems from several factors. First, with the exception of the first year after implementation, the number of crack offenders being released under a retroactivity policy would be essentially the same as under current practice. Therefore, there may be some issues of supervision for an expanded pool of offenders being released in year one, but after that there are no additional administrative issues involving offender supervision. Also, with the exception of a few districts such as the Eastern District of Virginia and the District of South Carolina, which would potentially have as many as 130–150 additional persons released during the first year, the vast majority of districts would experience an increase of well under 100 offenders during that period.

Second, criminological research on recidivism has generally not found any major differences in the degree of reoffending by time served in prison. That is, keeping offenders in prison for a longer period of time does not necessarily contribute significantly to reducing recidivism. A study by the Federal Bureau of Prisons documented the fiscal and public safety issues involved in assessing the value of time served in prison in the context of the advent of mandatory sentencing. Looking at a sample of drug sellers sentenced to prison in 1992 researchers concluded that 62% were considered low-risk

167

as measured by their criminal histories. The researchers then analyzed recidivism rates for a comparable group of 236 offenders released from prison in 1987 (prior to the adoption of guidelines and mandatory minimums) and found that only 19% of the low-risk offenders were rearrested within three years of release, and none for a violent offense. In contrast, as a result of sentencing changes, the low-risk traffickers sentenced to prison in 1992 were expected to serve about three years longer than the 1987 release group, at an estimated additional cost of $515 million.

These data apply to low-level offenders, but as the Department of Justice notes in its November 1st [2007] letter to the Commission, more serious offenders would also benefit from the sentence reductions. The Department notes that a recidivism study published by the Commission shows that "guideline offenders in higher CHCs [Criminal History Category] are more likely to re-offend within two years of release from prison or upon entering probation status," and that "offenders in CHC 1 have a substantially lower risk of recidivating within two years (13.8%) than do offenders in CHC VI (55.2%)."

Unfounded and Exaggerated Fears

The Department's concern, though, seriously overstates the extent of the problem involved. First, the Department fails to note from the Commission's prior research that two findings suggest the potential problem is not as great as argued. One is that many of these offenders will be well into their 40s and 50s, a period when recidivism rates typically decline sharply. For example, recidivism rates for persons over 40 in CHC VI are 41%, but are nonetheless one-third lower than for a comparable group in the age range of 26–35. The Commission data also demonstrate that persons convicted of drug trafficking offenses display a lower rate of recidivism than any other offense category, about 20% lower than for fraud and larceny, and 38% lower than for robbery.

Role Played Is More Important than Weight

If what we care about is prioritizing the capture of drug kingpins and key men, we need to stop using the false proxy of weight [of cocaine possessed]. Rather, we should base the mandatory minimums and the guidelines more directly on the role played by the defendant.

Some may object that the advantage of using weight as a proxy is that it is easy to measure and to incorporate into the system of sentencing. Although that is true, it is also true that we already incorporate role directly into the system. . . .

Our current system looks to weight to primarily set the sentence and then tinkers with the result in a much more minor way by considering role in the offense. This is odd, given that weight is being used largely as a proxy for role in the offense. My suggestion is that we flip these around and use the role in the offense as a principal sorting mechanism and weight of narcotics as a way to then adjust the result to differentiate between large and small operations.

Mark Osler,
Federal Sentencing Reporter,
June 2007.

The Department also argues that offenders sentenced from 1993 to 1995 are on average more likely than offenders sentenced in recent years to have a weapon involved in their offense or to have received an enhancement for obstruction of justice, and will also receive the greatest reductions in sentence under a retroactivity policy. These data are correct, but fail to note that this group of offenders will have served a minimum of 13–15 years by the time they are released, and in many cases, considerably longer periods of time. Thus, the Department's contention that the proposal "would result in the unexpected early return of serious drug dealers ... back into the community with the possibility of little or no re-entry preparation" points to the wrong problem. If the Department is concerned that after 15 years of incarceration they have not been able to prepare offenders for release to the community, how much time in fact would be required to do so? Further, few of these long-term offenders would be released immediately. For the vast majority there will be a period of at least 6–12 months, and in many cases five years or more, before the expiration of sentence. Surely this should allow sufficient time to implement whatever pre-release programming is normally provided to federal prison inmates prior to release.

Finally, it is important to note that under the proposal judges would not be obligated to reduce the prison term of any given offender. In cases where there may be concerns for public safety there will be ample opportunity to take these into consideration, and to let the original sentence stand if appropriate.

Righting Previous Wrongs

The vast majority of people who would be affected by a retro-activity policy have been sentenced since 1995, the year that the Sentencing Commission first reported on cocaine sentencing policy and recommended sentencing reform. Therefore, the Commission, as well as many legal groups and others, has been on record for this full period as supporting policies that are essentially consistent with a policy of retroactivity. It is therefore difficult to imagine a compelling rationale for not extending this long-awaited reform to the very group of offenders who would have benefited from any of the proposals recommended by the Commission in 1995 and subsequently.

As has been well documented, crack cocaine law enforcement and sentencing policies and practices have had a highly disproportionate effect on African Americans. Currently, more than 80% of the people prosecuted under the federal statutes are black. Whether or not this is evidence of bias in policy or practice, it clearly demonstrates that a retroactivity change would disproportionately benefit African Americans, with the Commission estimating the figure at 85%. Given that previous drug amendment changes adopted by the Commission benefited higher proportions of Hispanics and non-Hispanic whites, if the Commission did not apply the current proposal retroactively this would raise serious concerns about bias in public policy.

Reducing Prison Costs with Retroactive Policy

In its submission to the Commission, the Department of Justice raises concerns regarding the cost of implementing the retroactivity policy, ranging from transportation and housing by the U.S. Marshal's Service to panel attorneys to represent petitioners. While the Department provides no cost estimates for these functions aside from a figure of about $9 million for district court consideration of the cases, it is surprising that no mention is made of the fiscal impact on the Bureau of Prisons. Given that the Sentencing Commission's analysis shows that the average crack offender would receive a reduction of 27 months in prison, we can use a conservative annual figure of $23,000 for the cost of incarceration to project a potential savings of about $52,000 per prisoner. If in fact 19,000 prisoners received such reductions over a period of 30 years that would translate into a potential savings of about $1 billion.

I recognize, of course, that calculating cost savings in regard to incarceration involves an assessment of both fixed institutional costs and marginal costs per prisoner and is therefore a complex calculation. Nonetheless, the dramatic scale of potential savings suggests that long-term costs to the federal government for courts and corrections would be significantly reduced under the retroactivity proposal.

It is important to note as well that while it is not inappropriate to consider the fiscal costs of various sentencing policies, there are certain functions of the criminal justice system that are both expensive but necessary. For example, providing attorneys to indigent defendants is quite expensive, yet we do so because it is required by the Constitution. Similarly, when considering a policy of retroactivity, we should evaluate it on the merits of justice and public safety, and place a presumption in favor of an appropriate policy unless fiscal considerations are completely unreasonable.

Eliminating Burdens While Enhancing Justice

As we have indicated in our letter to the Commission, we believe that the crack cocaine amendment can be applied retroactively in a way that does not present a substantial administrative burden. We recognize, of course, that there will be an increased workload on the courts and Bureau of Prisons to a certain extent, but we also note that depriving persons of their liberty when there is no compelling state interest is a step that should not be taken lightly. We hope that the Commission can work with the courts and prison officials to implement a policy of retroactivity in a way that does not cause any undue burdens on these institutions. By doing so, the Commission will ensure that an important step toward enhancing equal justice is achieved.

"Without finality, the criminal law is deprived of much of its deterrent effect."

Crack Cocaine Sentencing Laws Should Not Be Reformed Retroactively

Gretchen C.F. Shappert

In the following viewpoint, Gretchen C.F. Shappert argues that amending crack cocaine sentencing laws retroactively will have an overall negative impact on the criminal justice system and the safety of U.S. citizens. She states that the communities most affected by crack cocaine-related crimes will suffer if crack cocaine offenders are released before the completion of their sentences, and the deterrent effect of long sentences for crack cocaine-related crimes will be reduced. While admitting that African Americans have been affected disproportionately by these sentencing laws enacted in 1986, Shappert maintains that many of the positive strides made in combating crime resulting from crack cocaine trafficking and use have been a direct result of these laws. Gretchen C.F. Shappert is U.S. attorney for the Western District of North Carolina.

Gretchen C.F. Shappert, "Statement before the U.S. Senate Committee on the Judiciary, Subcommitte on Crime and Drugs, 'Federal Cocaine Sentencing Laws: Reforming the 100–1 Crack/Powder Disparity,'" February 12, 2008.

As you read, consider the following questions:

1. What two conditions does Shappert believe crack co-caine sentencing reform must satisfy?

2. What percentages of powder cocaine offenders and crack cocaine offenders had access to, possession of, or used a weapon in their crimes, according to the 2007 United States Sentencing Commission Report on Crack Co-caine?

3. Why does Shappert think that offenders who are re-leased early would not benefit from the Bureau of Prisons' pre-release programs?

I have been in public service most of my professional life, both as a prosecutor and as an assistant public defender [in North Carolina]. [In February 2008] I completed 4[frac12] consecutive weeks of trial, including two trials in my district involving crack cocaine distribution. Indeed, much of my professional career has been defined by the ravages of crack cocaine, both as a defense attorney and as a prosecutor.

The Department of Justice recognizes that the penalty structure and quantity differentials for powder and crack cocaine created by Congress as part of the Anti-Drug Abuse Act of 1986 are seen by many as empirically unsupportable and unfair because of their disparate impact. As this subcommittee knows, since the mid-1990s, there has been a great deal of discussion and debate on this issue. There have been many proposals but little consensus on exactly how these statutes should be changed.

We remain committed to that effort today and are here in a spirit of cooperation to continue working toward a viable solution. We continue to insist upon working together on this issue that we get it right not just for offenders, but also for the law-abiding people whom we are sworn to serve and protect.

Revitalizing Communities Ravaged by Crack Cocaine

It has been said, and certainly it has been my experience, that whereas cocaine powder destroys an individual, crack cocaine destroys a community. The emergence of crack cocaine as the major drug of choice in Charlotte [North Carolina] during the late 1980's dramatically transformed the landscape. We saw an epidemic of violence, open-air drug markets, and urban terrorism unlike anything we had experienced previously. The sound of gunfire after dark was not uncommon in some communities. Families were afraid to leave their homes after dark and frightened individuals literally slept in their bathtubs to avoid stray bullets.

I have also seen the dramatic results when federal prosecutors, allied with local law enforcement and community leaders, make a commitment to take back neighborhoods from the gun-toting drug dealers who have laid claim to their communities. The successes of our Project Safe Neighborhoods (PSN) initiatives, combined with Weed & Seed, have literally transformed neighborhoods. In Shelby, North Carolina, for example, federal prosecutions of violent crack-dealing street gangs have slashed the crime rate and have enabled neighborhood groups to begin a community garden, truancy initiatives, and sports programs for young people. Traditional barriers are breaking down, and Shelby is thriving as an open and diverse small southern city. This transformation would not have been possible without an aggressive and collaborative approach to the systemic crack cocaine problem in that community.

In the jury trial I completed [in February 2008], the jury convicted the remaining two defendants in a seventy-person drug investigation that originated in the furniture manufacturing community of Lenoir, North Carolina. Several years ago, street drug dealers literally halted traffic to solicit crack cocaine customers in several Lenoir communities. At trial, the jury heard of an episode where drug dealers kidnapped and held for ransom one of their coconspirators, demanding repayment of a drug debt. After pistol-whipping their hostage, they finally released him. This is the kind of violent activity we have come to expect from crack cocaine traffickers, even in relatively tranquil small communities.

Protecting Law-Abiding Citizens

I am pleased to be able to tell you that we used the tools that Congress gave us to stop these dealers. We built strong cases against them. Local law enforcement officers, in conjunction with federal agents, have seized substantial quantities of crack and firearms from these dealers and dismantled their operations. It is a testament to the courage of people who live in these communities that they have been willing to cooperate with law enforcement and testify. Our most powerful witnesses are the citizens who have been victimized by crack-related violence. Cooperation from citizens in these communities is based upon their trust in our ability to prosecute these violent offenders successfully and send them away for lengthy federal prison sentences.

I know from my conversations with state and federal prosecutors from around the country that our experience in North Carolina is not unique or uncommon. When considering reforms to cocaine sentencing, we must never forget that honest, law-abiding citizens are also affected by what these dealers do. Unlike the men and women who chose to commit the crimes that terrorized our neighborhoods, the only choice many of the residents of these neighborhoods have is to rely on the criminal justice system to look out for them and their families. Let us make sure the rules we make at the federal level allow us to continue to do so.

Toward that end, we believe that any reform to cocaine sentencing must satisfy two important conditions. First, any reforms should come from the Congress and not the United

States Sentencing Commission. Second, any reforms, except in very limited circumstances, should apply only prospectively [i.e., not retroactively]. I will discuss the reasons necessitating each condition in turn.

A Job for Congress

First, bringing the expertise of the Congress to this issue will give the American people the best chance for a well-considered and fair result that takes into account not just the differential between crack and powder on offenders, but the implications of crack and powder cocaine trafficking on the communities and citizens whom we serve. Congress struck the present balance in 1986. Since then, although there have been many policy objections raised in debate, these statutes have been repeatedly upheld as constitutional. As a federal prosecutor, I have done my best to enforce these laws for the benefit of our communities.

Cleared of hyperbole, what we are talking about is whether the current balance between the competing interests in drug sentencing is appropriate. We are trying to ascertain what change will ensure that prosecutors have the tools to effectively combat drug dealers like those who terrorized western North Carolina while addressing the concerns about the present structure's disparate impact on African-American offenders. That is a decision for which Congress and this Subcommittee are made. At some level, the United States Sentencing Commission itself recognized that when it delayed retroactive implementation of the reduced crack cocaine guideline until March 3, 2008, thereby giving Congress a short window to review and consider the broader implications of their policy choice.

More Serious Crime Necessitates More Severe Penalties

In considering options, we continue to believe that a variety of factors fully justify higher penalties for crack offenses. In the cases I have prosecuted, I have seen the greater violence at the local level associated with the distribution of crack as compared to powder. United States Sentencing Commission data and reports confirm what I have seen, as they show that in federally prosecuted cases, crack offenders are more frequently associated with weapons use than powder cocaine offenders. According to the United States Sentencing Commission 2007 report on crack cocaine, powder cocaine offenders had access to, possession of, or used a weapon in 15.7 percent of cases in 2005. In contrast, crack cocaine offenders had access to, possession of, or used a weapon in 32.4 percent of cases in 2005.

That said, we understand that questions have been raised about the quantity differential between crack and powder cocaine, particularly because African-Americans constitute the vast majority of federal crack offenders. The Department of Justice is open to discussing possible reforms of the differential that are developed with victims and public safety as the foremost concerns, and that would both ensure no retreat from the success we have had fighting drug trafficking and simultaneously increase trust and confidence in the criminal justice system.

Retroactivity Undermines Deterrence

Second, reforms in this area, except in very limited circumstances, should apply prospectively. Notwithstanding the wide differences in the bills addressing the crack-powder differential, there is one great commonality. Across the board, they are all drafted to apply only prospectively.

Without finality, the criminal law is deprived of much of its deterrent effect. Even where the Supreme Court has found constitutional infirmities affecting fundamental rights of criminal defendants, it rarely has applied those roles retroactively. For example, the United States Supreme Court has not made its constitutional decision in *United States v. Booker*

Making Crack Cocaine Sentencing Amendments Retroactive Contradicts Congressional Decisions

Retroactive application of the crack amendment would, for the approximately 1,500 defendants who were sentenced between 1987 and 1995, overrule a Congressional vote denying reductions in their sentences as proposed by the Commission in 1995. The same might be said of those crack defendants who were sentenced between 1995 and 2002 when the Commission again suggested that Congress reduce the penalties for crack. For these two groups (approximately 6,500 or one-third of the estimated eligible defendants) Congress either specifically rejected a reduction in crack penalties or declined to intervene.

A decision by the Commission to make the amendment retroactive at this late date [2007] would be unreviewable by Congress absent extraordinary legislative action. This appears to run counter to the current prevailing sentiment evidenced by the three bills pending before the Senate that would reduce the penalties for crack. They either specifically reject or do not include authorization for retroactive application of their mandated change in the statutes. Thus, a decision to apply the amendments retroactively would be in discord with the past and current sentiments of Congress.

Alice Fisher, letter to Judge Ricardo H. Hinojosa of
the United States Sentencing Commission, November 1, 2007.

[which addresses the use of mandatory minimum sentences], the most fundamental change in sentencing law in decades, retroactive.

The shortcomings of retroactive application of new rules are illustrated starkly in the Sentencing Commission's recent decision to extend eligibility for its reduced crack penalty structure retroactively to more than 20,000 crack dealers already in prison.

Proponents of retroactivity argue that we should not be worried about the most serious and violent offenders being released too early because a federal judge will still have to decide whether to let such offenders out. But that misses an important point. The litigation and effort to make such decisions in so many cases forces prosecutors, probation officers, and judges to marshal their limited resources to keep in prison defendants whose judgments were already made final under the rules as all the parties understood them and reasonably relied on them to be.

The Burden on the Criminal Justice System

The swell of litigation triggered by the Commission's decision will affect different districts differently. Where it will have the most impact, however, will be in those districts that have successfully prosecuted the bulk of crack cases over the past two decades. Fifteen districts will bear a disproportionate 42.8 percent of the estimated eligible offenders. Similarly, more than 50 percent of the cases will have to be handled by the Fourth, Fifth, and Eleventh Circuits. The 536 estimated offenders in my district who are eligible for resentencing is the equivalent of 66 percent of all criminal cases handled in my district in 2006.

The litigation, furthermore, is likely to be greater than that envisioned by the Commission. Notwithstanding strict guidance to the contrary, the federal defenders already have issued guidance telling defense counsel to argue that the Supreme Court's decision in *United States v. Booker* applies and that, therefore, every court should consider not only the two-level reductions authorized by the Commission but conduct a full resentencing at which any and all mitigating evidence may be considered. If courts accept this argument, the administrative and litigation burden will far exceed the estimates the Commission relied upon in making their new rule retroactive and will create the anomalous result that only crack defendants— many of whom are among the most violent of all federal defendants—will get the benefit of the retroactive effect of *Booker*.

Releasing Those Most Likely to Re-offend

With retroactivity, many of these offenders, probably at least 1600 at a minimum, will be eligible for immediate release. Others will have their sentences cut in such a fashion that they may not have the full benefit of the Bureau of Prison's pre-release programs to prepare them to come back to their communities. I am deeply concerned that the success we are experiencing in some of our most fragile, formerly crack-ravaged communities will be seriously interrupted if these communities are forced to absorb a disproportionate number of convicted felons, who are statistically among the most likely persons to re-offend. . . .

The Federal Sentencing Guidelines assign to each offender one of six criminal history categories. The categorization is based upon the extent of an offender's past convictions and the recency of those convictions. Criminal History Category I is assigned to the least serious criminal record and includes many first-time offenders. Criminal History Category VI is the most serious category and includes offenders with the lengthiest criminal records. The Sentencing Commission's data shows that nearly 80 percent of the offenders who will be eligible for early release have a criminal history category of II or higher. Many of them will also have received an enhanced sentence because of a weapon or received a higher sentence because of their aggravating role in the offense.

Almost none of these offenders were new to the criminal justice system. The data shows that 65.2 percent of potentially eligible offenders had a criminal history category of III or higher. That fact alone tells us that these offenders will pose a much higher risk of recidivism upon their release.

The Sentencing Commission's 2004 recidivism study shows that offenders with a criminal history category of III have a 34.2 percent chance of recidivating within the first two years of their release. Those with criminal history category of VI have a 55.2 percent chance of recidivating within the first two years of their release.

Reducing the Positive Impact of Re-Entry Programs

Our concern about the early release of these offenders is amplified by the fact that retroactive application of the crack amendment would result in many prisoners being unable to participate in specific pre-release programs provided by the Bureau of Prisons (BOP). Preparation to reenter society intensifies as the inmate gets closer to release. As part of this process, BOP provides a specific release preparation program and works with inmates to prepare a variety of documents that are needed upon release, such as a resume, training certificates, education transcripts, a driver's license, and a social security card. BOP also helps the inmate identify a job and a place to live. Finally, many inmates receive specific pre-release services afforded through placement in residential re-entry centers at the end of their sentences.

With no adjustments to BOP's prisoner re-entry processes, any reductions in sentence such as those contemplated by the retroactive application of the guideline may reduce or eliminate inmates' participation in the Bureau's re-entry programs. Without that, the offender's chance of re-offending will likely increase.

The Department of Justice is open to addressing the differential between crack and powder penalties as part of an effort to resolve the retroactivity issue. It is our hope that as we work together we can make sure that there is no retreat in the fight against drug trafficking and no loss in the public's trust and confidence in our criminal justice system.

Periodical Bibliography

The following articles have been selected to supplement the diverse views presented in this chapter.

Roy D. Adler and
Michael Summers
"Capital Punishment Works," *Wall Street Journal*, November 2, 2007.

Louis Freedberg
"Reforming Three Strikes," *Nation*, November 1, 2004.

Annette Fuentes
"Give the Kids a Break," *USA Today*, February 13, 2008.

Cathleen Kaveny
"Justice or Vengeance," *Commonweal*, February 15, 2008.

Nancy Merritt,
Terry Fain, and
Susan Turner
"Oregon's Get Tough Sentencing Reform: A Lesson in Justice System Adaptation," *Criminology & Public Policy*, February 2006.

Michael M. O'Hear
"The Second Chance Act and the Future of Reentry Reform," *Federal Sentencing Reporter*, December 2007.

Mary Price
"Mandatory Minimums in the Federal System: Turning a Blind Eye to Justice," *Human Rights: Journal of the Section of Individual Rights & Responsibilities*, Winter 2004.

Julie Rawe
"Congress's Bad Drug Habit," *Time*, November 19, 2007.

Bruce Shapiro
"A Lethal Decision," *Nation*, May 12, 2008.

Jonathan Turley
"The Punishment Fits the Times," *USA Today*, January 16, 2008.

Robert Weisberg
and Marc L. Miller
"Sentencing Lessons," *Stanford Law Review*, October 2005.

Are Defendants' Rights Protected in the United States?

Chapter Preface

As a result of the 1966 U.S. Supreme Court case of *Miranda v. Arizona*, law enforcement officers are obliged to warn suspects under arrest that they have the right to remain silent because anything said might be used as evidence in court, and that they have the right to an attorney—either self appointed or court appointed. This warning, known popularly as the Miranda warning, was designed to make all arrestees aware of their Fifth Amendment right to avoid self-incrimination during any police interrogation that could be considered coercive. The Miranda warning has remained a fixture of arrests ever since, and as law professor Mark A. Godsey notes, "In spite of forty years of legal developments and practical experience, the content of [the warning] has never been modified or even been subjected to systematic scrutiny."

In his 2006 article for the *Minnesota Law Review*, Godsey argues that the Miranda warning should be modified—or more accurately should evolve—to keep pace with changing legal principles and practical experiences. Godsey does not advocate disposing of Fifth Amendment protections, but he does call for updating them. He states that following the initial "You have the right to remain silent" warning should be the addendum, "If you choose to remain silent, your silence will not be used against you as evidence to suggest that you committed a crime simply because you refused to speak." Godsey goes on,

> Next, the [warnings] relating to the right to counsel, should be removed and replaced with three new requirements, reflecting legal developments and practical lessons that have come to light since 1966. The first requirement would be a new warning as follows: "If you choose to talk, you may change your mind and remain silent at any time, even if you have already spoken." The second requirement would be a

rule mandating that the police reinstruct suspects of the new Miranda warnings at intervals throughout lengthy interrogations. Finally, the police would be required to videotape interrogations.

Godsey suggests these alterations to the Miranda warning would ensure that suspects' rights were more adequately protected in light of modern police methods as well as legal theories that have reconceived defendants' rights.

Videotaping interrogations, as Godsey suggests, might ensure that at least some suspects were informed of their Miranda rights, but as many critics have noted, Miranda rights are only valuable when they are issued and when they are heeded. Popular crime author and lawyer Scott Turow contends that many individuals in his home city of Chicago are arrested without being issued Miranda warnings. He also states that in his 22 years of legal practice only one case that he dealt with was overturned based on inadmissible testimony due to a police officer failing to issue a Miranda warning. "Nor is my experience idiosyncratic," Turow writes in his June 2000 *New York Times* article. "After a couple of hours of computer research, I could not find a single reported decision in Illinois in the last 12 months in which a confession was suppressed or a conviction reversed because of a Miranda violation."

In the following chapter, other legal analysts and commentators examine various defendants' rights to determine if these protections are being safeguarded. Many of these rights are being formulated and redefined to meet current needs and situations, making Godsey's arguments applicable. But as Turow and some of the authors in this chapter point out, defendants' rights are only likely to be protective when they are utilized and not infringed.

> "The detainees at Guantánamo have been waiting for their day in federal court since January 2002, when the first petitions of habeas corpus, were filed."

War Detainees Deserve the Right to Habeas Corpus

Aziz Huq

In the following viewpoint, Aziz Huq argues that detainees captured in the United States' "war on terror" deserve the writ of habeas corpus to challenge their detention in a court of law. According to Huq, the government has fought to deny detainees this basic right and so far neither the courts nor the legislature have been helpful in procuring it. Huq asserts that the branches of government should work together to provide this check against unlawful detention, especially because America's allies are defending this right. Aziz Huq directs the Liberty and National Security Project at the Brennan Center for Justice, a public policy institute at the New York University School of Law.

As you read, consider the following questions:

1. What strategies has the U.S. government used to delay rulings on the right to habeas corpus for detainees, in Huq's view?

Aziz Huq, "Habeas Corpus Can't Wait," *TomPaine.com*, March 5, 2007. Reproduced by permission.

2. As Huq describes, what is Camp Six?

3. What two countries does Huq say have refused to pass more stringent counterterrorism detention laws?

[In February 2007], the Court of Appeals for the District of Columbia acted to return Guantánamo detainees [775 "enemy combatants" arrested by the U.S. armed forces in the Middle East and brought to this dentention center in Cuba] to the Supreme Court. They ruled against the detainees, holding that they have no rights under the Constitution, thanks to the Military Commissions Act of 2006 [which granted power to military commissions to try war detainees].

Partisans of the rule of law look forward to the High Court's intervention, expecting the court to rule for the detainees on the bottom-line question (of a right to writ of *habeas corpus*, or the right to challenge one's detention). Many in Congress will be tempted to hang back now and allow the federal courts to finally rule on the pivotal issues presented by cases, which first filed more than five years ago.

But we should not give in to the temptation to let the court pick up the slack for a legislature that has singularly failed to live up to its oversight responsibilities. Whether or not a court finds that the detainees have constitutional rights cannot and will not answer the many difficult questions raised by the detainees' predicament. And there is much that Congress can and must do, regardless of how the court rules.

The Right to Challenge One's Detention

The detainees at Guantánamo have been waiting for their day in federal court since January 2002, when the first petitions of *habeas corpus* were filed. From the beginning, the relief they sought has been narrow: not the automatic right to walk free, but the right to challenge the factual basis of their detention before an independent decision-maker. From the beginning of the Guantánamo regime, it has been clear that government claims that the camps housed "the worst of the worst" were factually wrong—and that the government knew as much.

This, however, is an administration that does cakewalks, not climbdowns.

Delay in the day of reckoning occurred not due to the detainees' lawyers, but through a series of increasingly reckless maneuvers by the administration and its lawyers to avoid any review of the factual grounds for detention. First the government argued that Guantánamo was not part of the United States, and the president's sweeping judgment that anyone picked up by the CIA from Bosnia to Pakistan via Thailand must be an "enemy combatant," and therefore undeserving of any judicial solicitude. Then there were legislative efforts, in the form of the 2005 Detainee Treatment Act and the 2006 Military Commissions Act, to stymie review.

It is important again to emphasize that what the government has sought to avoid is not simple "release." What the D.C. Circuit held last week was that the Military Commissions Act stripped the courts of power even to hear the detainees' pleas. And at best the Supreme Court will determine that the detainees have a right under the Constitution to be heard. None will necessarily be released. None will even immediately get a day in court. The best case scenario is that the mere prospect of review will push the government into moving forward with releases.

A Comprehensive Solution Is Needed

But this is not enough. To understand why, look at the section of Guantánamo called Camp Six. Camp Six is the "more comfortable" facility in which detainees who have been "cleared" are held. As James Cohen's . . . account for the *National Law Journal* makes clear, detainees in Camp Six are kept in cells with walls, floors and ceilings of solid metal for 22 hours a day, denied natural light or air and have virtually no contact

Habeas Corpus Is Not Much to Ask For

The right to habeas corpus is a limited right. Habeas does not give a person the right to a trial. It does not give a habeas petitioner a right to personally appear in court, and it most certainly does not mean that U.S. servicemen and women will be pulled from the battlefield to testify in such proceedings. All the government must do to defeat a habeas claim is demonstrate to a judge by a preponderance of the evidence that the detainee is being lawfully held. Most habeas petitions are rejected by the federal courts without the need to call a single witness. In fact, habeas petitions can be, and routinely are, disposed of in federal court based on a single affidavit by a government agent explaining the basis for detention. Habeas simply provides an opportunity for a detainee to argue to an independent federal judge that he or she is being held in error. If the detainee is properly held, this is a claim the government can easily overcome.

Patrick Leahy, Senate Statement on Amendment 2022,
the Habeas Corpus Restoration Act of 2007, September 19, 2007.

with human beings other than guards. Conditions are worse than any Supermax facility in the United States.

Thus, it is not sufficient to ensure that the detainees have their day in court. Even those who the government concedes to be innocent of any terrorist involvement are still kept in brutalizing and inhumane conditions. A comprehensive solution to the Guantánamo problem requires much more. And, acting alone, the courts have only limited capacity to that end.

So Congress too must act, and there is much that it can do now. The court proceedings are no cause for delay. A comprehensive solution necessarily involves multiple branches of government, and the sooner legislators act, the sooner America can remove the moral stain of Guantánamo from its plate.

Yet action will not be easy. With the Senate in Democratic hands by only a slim margin, and with no means of stopping filibusters [a filibuster is the blocking of a legislative vote by running out the time clock], the chances of enacting a comprehensive solution to the global detention problem are nonexistent. At best, this Congress may redress some of the worst aspects of the Military Commissions Act of 2006. As [independent nonprofit organization] Human Rights Watch indicated in its ... "Common Sense Agenda" for Congress, restoration of the "Great Writ" of *habeas corpus* ought to be at the top of the list of must-dos.

Mobilizing Democratic Institutions

Two bills introduced by Senator Christopher Dodd, and Senators Arlen Specter and Patrick Leahy, do this in whole or in part. The Dodd bill is more comprehensive, and its provision on restoring *habeas* is more carefully drafted.

Nevertheless, whether these bills pass or not, there is vital oversight work that the Judiciary, Armed Services and Intelligence Committees have been tardy in doing these five years. It is these committees, as much as the courts, that have the constitutional power to shine a light on Guantánamo.

There are many who will be hesitant about leaving much to the democratic branches. In theory, democratic bodies should respond best to majorities, and sideline minority concerns. (In practice, to be sure, well-organized and financed minorities, such as industrial lobbies, often yield unwarranted clout—but that is the result of America's eccentric belief in privatized campaign financing). Worse, minorities who lack representation, and who are the subject of racial animus, will be the brunt of cumulatively bad measures.

Without question, the immigration and counter-terrorism debates evince this dangerous dynamic. Nevertheless, the experience of other countries gives hope that democratic majorities can do better.

Other Nations Stand Up for Due Process

[In February 2007], the Canadian Supreme Court invalidated an indefinite detention scheme because it failed to provide procedural protections to ensure accurate determinations of dangerousness. If the American experience provides a general guide, this should have prompted massive retaliation, just as the *Hamdan v. Rumsfeld* [which argued that military commissions violate statutory law] decision provoked the Military Commissions Act.

Instead, the Canadian House of Commons voted down, 159 votes to 124, the renewal of two provisions of an antiterrorism bill that allowed warrantless detention for brief periods. The Canadian legislature focused on the record of counter-terrorism measures over the past five years and concluded the two provisions were unwarranted infringements on human liberties.

The British Parliament too has shown spine in the face of government fearmongering. In November 2005, in the wake of the [London] 7/7 bombings, the Blair government proposed an extension of counterterrorism preventative detention from 14 days to 90 days. Despite heavy lobbying from the Metropolitan Police, the measure was defeated 391–322. It is especially striking that the British Parliament was able to focus on the real issues of proportionality and due process.

Congress can do just as well as its common-law cousins. We the people must now hold it up to their high standards.

> "Aliens with no immigration status who are captured and held outside the territorial jurisdiction of the United States, and whose only connection to our country is to wage a barbaric war against it, do not have any rights, much less 'basic rights,' under our Constitution."

War Detainees Have No Right to Habeas Corpus

Andrew C. McCarthy

In the following viewpoint, Andrew C. McCarthy asserts that those who believe the detainees captured in the United States' "war on terror" deserve the writ of habeas corpus are mistaken. McCarthy claims that alien detainees have no rights recognized by the U.S. Constitution or Congress and therefore do not have the right to challenge their detention in the courts. Despite the fact that habeas corpus is not granted by U.S. law, McCarthy assures that it is granted in principle at the military commissions used to try detainees. Andrew C. McCarthy is a senior fellow at

Andrew C. McCarthy, "The New Detainee Law Does Not Deny Habeas Corpus," *National Review*, October 3, 2006. Copyright © 2006 by National Review, Inc., 215 Lexington Avenue, New York, NY 10016. Reproduced by permission.

the Foundation for the Defense of Democracies, an anti-terrorism organization that promotes research and education on policy issues.

As you read, consider the following questions:

1. According to McCarthy, why did the Supreme Court rule in *Hamdan v. Rumsfeld* that the Geneva Conventions Common Article 3 applied to detainees?
2. What does the author say is the proper course for nations to protest the detention of citizens captured by the United States during the war on terror?
3. In what way does the Detainee Treatment Act essentially grant habeas corpus privileges, in McCarthy's view?

There are innumerable positives in the Military Commissions Act of 2006, the new law on the treatment of enemy combatants that President [George W.] Bush [signed in October 2006]. Among the best is Congress's refusal to grant habeas-corpus rights to alien terrorists. After all, the terrorists already have them.

That the critique on this entirely appropriate measure has been dead wrong is given away by its full-throated hysteria. Typical was Richard Epstein, a distinguished constitutional law professor at the University of Chicago, who admonished the Senate Judiciary Committee that the Bush administration and a compliant Republican Congress were unconstitutionally "suspend[ing]" the great writ. The *New York Times* editorial board, in its signature hyperbole, railed that "[d]etainees in U.S. military prisons would lose the basic right to challenge their imprisonment." What bunkum.

Al Qaeda Terrorists Have No Constitutional Rights

First, Congress cannot "suspend" habeas corpus by denying it to people who have no right to it in the first place. The right against suspension of habeas corpus is found in the Constitution (art. I, 9). Constitutional rights belong only to Americans—that is, according to the Supreme Court, U.S. citizens and those aliens who, by lawfully weaving themselves into the fabric of our society, have become part of our national community (which is to say, lawful permanent resident aliens). To the contrary, aliens with no immigration status who are captured and held outside the territorial jurisdiction of the United States, and whose only connection to our country is to wage a barbaric war against it, do not have *any* rights, much less "basic rights," under our Constitution.

Indeed, even when the Supreme Court, in its radical 2004 *Rasul* [*v. Bush*] case [a 2004 U.S. Supreme Court case in which the courts stipulated that they had the power to hear wrongful imprisonment pleas from detainees], opened the courthouse doors to enemy fighters in wartime for the first time in American history, it relied not on the Constitution but on the *federal habeas corpus statute.* So put aside that *Rasul* was an exercise in judicial legerdemain whose holding depended on a distortion of both that statute and the long-established limitations on the Court's own jurisdiction (which does not extend outside sovereign U.S. territory to places like Guantanamo Bay, Cuba). Even in its willful determination to reach a result that rewarded al Qaeda's lawfare, the Court declined to rule that alien combatants have fundamental habeas rights. Instead, they have only what Congress chooses to give them—which Congress can change at any time.

Al Qaeda Terrorists Have No Treaty Rights

But wait. Isn't habeas corpus necessary so that the terrorists can press the Geneva Convention rights with which the Court most recently vested them in its 2006 *Hamdan* [*v. Rumsfeld*] case? Wrong again.

To begin with, although its reasoning was murky, the *Hamdan* majority seems technically to have held that Geneva's Common Article 3 applied to military commissions because

The Military Commissions Act of 2006 Nullifies Recourse to Habeas Corpus

In General.—Section 2241 of title 28, United States Code, is amended by striking both the subsection (e) added by section 1005(e)(1) of Public Law 109-148 (119 Stat. 2742) and the subsection (e) added by section 1405(e)(1) of Public Law 109-163 (119 Stat. 3477) and inserting the following new subsection (e):

"(e)(1) No court, justice, or judge shall have jurisdiction to hear or consider an application for a writ of habeas corpus filed by or on behalf of an alien detained by the United States who has been determined by the United States to have been properly detained as an enemy combatant or is awaiting such determination.

"(2) Except as provided in paragraphs (2) and (3) of section 1005(e) of the Detainee Treatment Act of 2005 (10 U.S.C. 801 note), no court, justice, or judge shall have jurisdiction to hear or consider any other action against the United States or its agents relating to any aspect of the detention, transfer, treatment, trial, or conditions of confinement of an alien who is or was detained by the United States and has been determined by the United States to have been properly detained as an enemy combatant or is awaiting such determination."

Military Commissions Act of 2006,
Public Law 109-366, October 17, 2006.

of a congressional statute, the Uniform Code of Military Justice. Again, if a right is rooted in a statute, not in the Constitution, Congress is at liberty to withdraw or alter the right simply by enacting a new statute. Such a right is not in any sense "basic."

But don't some human-rights activists contend the *Hamdan* ruling means Common Article 3 [which covers treatment of non-combatant detainees] applies not just because of a statute but because of its own force as part of a treaty that the United States has ratified? Well, yes, they do make that claim—and . . . they have gotten plenty of help from the recent debate prompted by Senators John McCain, Lindsey Graham, and others who insisted *Hamdan* meant Common Article 3 controls interrogation practices.

Even with all of that, though, it remains a settled principle that treaties are compacts between sovereign nations, not fonts of individual rights. Alleged violations are thus grist for diplomacy, not litigation. Treaties are not judicially enforceable by individuals absent an express statement to the contrary in the treaty's text. By contrast, Geneva's express statements indicate that no judicial intervention was contemplated. . . .

Consequently, *if* Congress had actually denied al Qaeda detainees a right to use Common Article 3 to challenge their detention in federal court (and, as we'll soon see, Congress has not done that), that would merely have reaffirmed what has been the law for over a half century.

If the political representatives of a nation believe one of its citizens is being unlawfully held at Gitmo [Guantanamo Bay], the proper procedure is for that nation to protest to our State Department, not for the detainee to sue our country in our courts. In fact, several nations have made such claims, and the Bush administration has often responded by repatriating detainees to their home countries . . . only to have many of them rejoin the jihad. In any event, though, there would be nothing wrong with declining to allow habeas to be used for the creation of individual rights that detainees do not in fact have under international law.

Al Qaeda Terrorists *Do* Get to Challenge Their Detention

But let's ignore that the critics are wrong about the entitlement of al Qaeda terrorists to constitutional or treaty-based rights to habeas. There is an even more gaping hole in their attack on the new law. *Congress has already given al Qaeda detainees the very rights the critics claim have been denied.*

[In] December [2005], Congress enacted the Detainee Treatment Act (DTA). It requires that the military must grant each detainee a Combatant Status Review Tribunal (CSRT) at which to challenge his detention. Assuming the military's CSRT process determines he is properly detained, the detainee then has a right to appeal to our civilian-justice system—specifically, to the U.S. Court of Appeals for the D.C. Circuit. And if that appeal is unsuccessful, the terrorist may also seek certiorari [court record] review by the Supreme Court.

This was a revolutionary innovation. As we've seen, *Rasul* did not (and could not) require Congress to allow enemy combatants access to the federal courts. Congress could lawfully have responded to *Rasul* by amending the habeas statute to make clear that al Qaeda terrorists have no more right to petition our courts in wartime than any other enemy prisoners have had in the preceding two-plus centuries. Instead, Congress responded by giving the enemy what are in every meaningful way habeas rights.

For the enemy combatants, habeas corpus, to borrow the [*New York*] *Times*'s articulation, is simply a "right to challenge their imprisonment" in federal court. So what does the DTA do? It allows a detainee who has been found by the military to be properly held as an enemy combatant to challenge his incarceration in federal court. Under DTA section 1005(e)(2), that court (the D.C. Circuit) is expressly empowered to determine whether the detention is in violation of the Constitution and laws of the United States—which, of course, include treaties to whatever extent they may create individual rights.

The DTA Rules Have Been Clarified by the Military Commissions Act

Thus, the DTA has already granted to our enemies the very remedy critics claim is now being denied. Moreover, the new Military Commissions Act (MCA) does not repeal the DTA. It strengthens it. That is, because the Supreme Court's *Hamdan* decision created confusion about whether the DTA was meant to apply retroactively to the 400-plus habeas petitions that were already filed, the MCA clarifies that all detainees who wish to challenge their imprisonment must follow the DTA procedure for doing so. But, importantly, the right to challenge imprisonment is itself reaffirmed.

That the DTA does not refer to this right as *habeas corpus* is irrelevant. It's not the name of the remedy that counts; it's the substance. The DTA gives the detainee exactly what habeas provides. Therefore, it would have been pointless for the MCA to add yet another round of habeas.

To understand why this is so, one need only consider the legal restrictions on imprisoned American citizens. If they wish to claim their detention is baseless, they are not permitted to file habeas petitions which simply re-allege claims they have already made (or at least had a fair opportunity to make) during prior legal proceedings (such as the appeal of a criminal conviction, or a previously filed habeas petition). Repetitious claims are instantly disregarded by courts as a form of procedural default known as "abuse of the writ" of habeas corpus.

Given that habeas would not be available to *an American* for the purpose of rehashing a previously unsuccessful challenge to his imprisonment, why on earth should we extend habeas to *an alien al Qaeda terrorist* so he can re-litigate under the MCA an argument against his detention that has already been heard and rejected by a federal appeals court under the DTA?

The Folly of Criticism

Epstein's arguments are especially unbecoming. First, for all his bombast about the storied history of the habeas writ, he neglects to mention that the thousands upon thousands of alien enemy combatants our military has detained outside the U.S. in the long history of American warfare have never had a right to challenge their detention by calling on the judicial branch of our government at the very time the political branches have taken our nation into battle. It was *Rasul* that broke with tradition here. Even if enemy combatants had been denied habeas in this war—which, of course, has not happened—that would not have been a departure from tradition at all.

Second, it is simply preposterous to suggest, as Epstein does, that the government is likely to frustrate the DTA's judicial review procedure by such shenanigans as starting a CSRT but then suspending it indefinitely without ruling on a detainee's status (so the DTA right to appeal to the D.C. Circuit would never be triggered). The DTA not only directed the Defense Department to come up with CSRT procedures, including an annual review of the status of detainees found to be enemy combatants; it expressly contemplated oversight by the Armed Services committees in both Houses of Congress. There is no basis to believe either that the Pentagon is engaged in the kind of gamesmanship Epstein imagines or that Congress would tolerate such antics were they to occur.

It would be the height of folly to confer additional rights on alien enemy combatant terrorists—which, by the way, would be far better rights than honorable alien enemy combatants who do not mass-murder civilians get under the Geneva Conventions—for no better reason than to prevent an abuse that is virtually inconceivable in the real world. Such thinking reflects the same September 10th mentality that gave us the Justice Department's infamous "wall"—which prevented criminal investigators and national security agents from pooling threat information in order to forfend hypothetical and empirically unheard-of civil-rights violations.

Been there done that.

> *"Public defenders not only do a disservice to their clients by providing insufficient and incomprehensible legal representation, but they also yell at their clients if their clients dare try to demand more."*

Public Defenders Are Failing to Safeguard the Rights of Poor Defendants

Kirsten Anderberg

In the following viewpoint, Kirsten Anderberg argues that public defenders—attorneys appointed to defendants who cannot afford their own—should go on strike to bring attention to the problems these lawyers face. Anderberg asserts that public defenders are underpaid and overworked, and this stress is affecting their relationships with clients. Anderberg claims that public defenders cannot afford to spend a lot of time with individual clients because of their high caseloads, and that the lack of attention is leaving clients without adequate defense. Kirsten Anderberg is a graduate student in history who hopes to return to law school.

As you read, consider the following questions:

1. According to Philip Dawdy, as quoted by Anderberg, why did officials in King County, Washington, approve a $1 million cut to public defense funds in 2004?

2. How was Anderberg treated by a SCRAP public defender during her pretrial consultation?

3. According to Anderberg, what is the maximum number of cases a public defender in King County, Washington, may have per year?

The situation with underfunded public defenders, and plea bargains being thrown around more often than not, with poor people caught in the mix, denied the rights given them legally, to fair and proper representation, needs to stop. Now. This is no longer a situation where public defenders can stand around and keep pointing fingers at those funding them, usually the state. At a certain point, public defenders become accomplices in these crimes against the poor of inadequate, insufficient, incomprehensible, defense for serious crimes in America's Criminal Justice System. Something must be done and I think what needs to be done is public defenders need to go on strike. Seriously. Or else they are now accomplices. In Washington State's Superior Courts, about 85 to 90 percent of defendants tried on felony charges are considered low-income, and therefore entitled to court-appointed counsel. So this affects almost every person charged with a felony in the criminal justice system. Public defenders take out their frustrations and anger about being overworked and underfunding on innocent clients who just want to understand what is going on with their cases. It is no longer acceptable for public defenders to keep pretending they are giving a service all agree they are not. It appears quite standard knowledge that if you use a public defender, you have a much, much greater chance of going to jail than if you use a private attorney. And looking at who is actually charged with felonies, one can only surmise that you have a greater chance of being *charged* with a felony *if* you are poor, as the prosecutor immediately sees he will be dealing with insufficient representation from public defenders, and sees that a plea bargain will be easy. None of these things are the fault of the poor who get entrapped in the criminal justice system. It is the duty of the courts to provide fair and equal representation to the poor. That goal has failed in America with flying colors.

Underfunded and Stressed

In a [December 2004] article by Philip Dawdy in the *Seattle Weekly*, he says that the Metropolitan King County Council has approved a $1 million cut in the county's public-defense system for 2005. Dawdy calls the public defender system that just received these cuts "a traditionally underfunded program that provides court-appointed attorneys for low-income and indigent people accused of crimes." Dawdy says that one of the contracted non-profit public defense law firms that the county works with, Northwest Defenders, will be running at a deficit next year, due to the 2005 budget and may need to fold. And do not think that that stress remains within the locked boardrooms of the Northwest Defenders Association either. No, it comes spilling out onto the phone and into the hallways of the County's Courthouses as well. The clients are yelled at for wanting to understand their cases. The clients are barked at and told to be quiet and speak when spoken to, while in the middle of serious legal battles, as these public defenders yell at clients that they are overworked and they have more clients than they can handle. I have seen this behavior from employees and public defenders in King County with my own eyes.

When I worked at the Kent County Law Library, I had many mothers come in with swollen red eyes, asking me to explain the charges that just incarcerated their sons. I was given explicit instructions by the law library staff that I *may not* explain any charges to people who ask like that, as it was considered horning in on the legal field, as legal advice. So, the best I could do was lead these desperate women to books that explained the crimes in as close to plain English as possible. It broke my heart that women were losing their children, and public defenders did not even have the time to explain to the mothers what the actual charges meant or what was going on. These public defenders not only do a disservice to their clients by providing insufficient and incomprehensible legal representation, but they also yell at their clients if their clients dare try to demand more. This is not a healthy situation for anyone, and it certainly is not blind justice by any stretch.

Something Must Be Done

Dawdy's article says that county officials approved the $1 million cut to public defense because they predict they will be handling less complex aggravated-murder cases in 2005, and they predict that prosecutors will be charging minor felonies as misdemeanors. And even if those were believable reasons to predict less need for funds in 2005, that does not take into account the glaring reality that the public defense agencies have been functioning below par for years now, and something must be done. If the need for services was reduced, and funding stayed the same, then maybe, just maybe, we could move one half step forward towards getting some equal representation in courtrooms in Washington's criminal injustice system. But it ain't happening anytime soon.

Dawdy's article quotes a City Council member saying, "Our system of justice is tremendously weakened when we fail to live up to our promise for a fair and competent defense for all who stand accused of a crime." So, apparently these people *get it.* They just do not want to actually do anything *about it.* The trail of complaints from clients and public defenders themselves about this terrible situation is long and public. . . .

Inadequate Counsel Leads to Wrongful Convictions

Without advocates, some poor defendants serve jail time longer than the law requires or plead guilty to crimes they didn't commit just to get out of jail. A few, as has been documented, receive the death penalty or life in prison because their court-appointed lawyers were incompetent, lazy, or both. Most shocking, says Norman Lefstein, who chaired the American Bar Association's Indigent Defense Advisory Group, "is the lack of overall real success, the lack of progress" given the overwhelming evidence that inadequate counsel often leads to wrongful conviction. The many cases we know about "likely are only the tip of the iceberg," he says. "This is an enormous problem."

Kit R. Roane, U.S. News & World Report, January 15, 2006.

Poorly Serving Clients

I remember very clearly, and have written in that day's notes, an incident where an employee named Sam with SCRAP [Society of Counsel Representing Accused Persons], a King County Public Defender agency, yelled at *me* because *she* said she had "64 people (we) represent and you will not see me until the hearing date. If you do not like it, hire an attorney." I remember this woman Sam pacing the floor outside the courtroom, taking out her angers and hostilities on clients, not the state or people who created that system, but instead on us, the indigent she was organizing the representation of. That day, I watched Sam play stupid games over and over due to her annoyance with her caseload. When I first arrived, I asked Sam, whom I did not know or recognize, as she would not meet with me before my actual hearing (!), but she looked like authority and had files, so I asked her if she knew where the list of who was on that day's SCRAP roster was. She quipped I needed to go to the 12th floor. I asked if she was a SCRAP attorney. She said yes. I said they were representing me, so could she tell me if I was on that day's SCRAP representation roster. Her response was, "No, only the attorney can tell you that." As I said, I took notes in the courthouse of her actions. I told her I was never told who my attorney WAS, nor had I met them to my dismay, so I only knew SCRAP as my defenders that day. She said I would have to talk to my attorney! I repeated I did not know who that was, so if she worked for SCRAP, could she please tell me WHO my attorney was so I could ask HIM/HER if I was on the roster, since this is apparently some kind of needle in a haystack game. She said my attorney would call my name eventually if I was on the roster. . . . Is this type of treatment of clients necessary? Would I continue to employ a private attorney who represented me in such a fashion? No way.

The Consequences of an Inadequate Defense

In a *Seattle Times* article from May 2004, by Ken Armstrong, entitled, "State Bar-Association Panel Urges Public-Defense Reforms," it cites indigent defendants who have been "poorly served, even victimized, by those entrusted with protecting their civil rights," according to a report just released by a Washington State Bar Association panel. The article goes on to say, "The panel, whose 17 members include judges from the Washington Supreme Court on down, calls for new laws or court rules to address a litany of problems, including a lack of enforceable standards for public-defense lawyers, inadequate funding and the proliferation of fixed-fee public-defense contracts that invite abuse. . . . Some individuals and private firms profit from public-defense contracts while providing minimal or substandard representation to their clients, and many in positions to know of these failures look away as defendants' constitutional rights to effective assistance of counsel are denied," the panel's report says. That report was given to the Board of Governors in May 2004. So how is it that $1 million was just cut from that budget?

In Armstrong's article, he says that this [Washington] State Bar Association panel also wrote that the consequences of an inadequate defense "can be devastating for the individuals whose liberty is at stake, for the legal system, and for society as a whole." He cites problems with the public defender system showing up as "wrongful convictions, appeals and retrials at added taxpayer expense, civil-rights lawsuits and a loss of respect for the courts." The Bar Association report also says, "Public trust and confidence in Washington's judges and court system suffer when the public perceives that individuals charged with crimes are treated unfairly."

Armstrong's article says that "the panel's call for reform is the latest in a long line of such reports, which go back three decades and include criticism of Washington's public-defense system from legislative committees, bar groups and legal-research organizations." He quotes a member of the Washington State Office of Public Defense saying, "It's been said over and over again in Washington—some attorneys providing public-defense representation are inadequately paid, lack experience and other qualifications, and have such enormous caseloads that they literally don't have time to perform the tasks necessary for adequate representation." The same article quotes Supreme Court Justice Susan Owens, as saying many public defenders do good work, but in general, "They are overworked. They are underpaid."

Armstrong's article said that "*The Seattle Times* published a series last month on the chronic failures of Washington's public-defense system, revealing such shortcomings as staggering caseloads that make it all but impossible for many defense attorneys to do their job effectively." Armstrong cites one of the caseload problems in King County is the "fixed-fee contracts" with public defense firms, as that discourages them from investing proper time as they get paid the same for cases whether they invest in a case's complexity or not. The report from the Bar Association in May 2004 said, according to Armstrong's article, that "local governments should be required to implement meaningful public-defense standards, and should be prohibited from renewing contracts with attorneys who have failed to provide an effective defense."

Untrained and Unsupervised

One of the most glaring and obvious inequity factors involved with public defense representation is that most prosecutors are paid approximately two times the salary of public defenders, and they also are given full reign of the state's resources such as the police dept.'s investigators, etc., which are things that public defenders need to do outside contracting for. As a matter of fact, in my little romp with inadequate representation by public defenders in Seattle, the "investigator" in my case was a woman with no prior investigative experience, who was using this "internship" with a public defenders group for a new life experience . . . ugh. I did work as a private investigator for years, and watching her bumble about, when my case was at stake, was unbelievable. In the end, not a thing she did was of use. In the end, the public defender in my King County case stood up in front of the judge and said, "Your honor, if Ms. Anderberg had had proper legal representation, she would not be here today." So hmmm, what was *he* again? Amazing stuff! So we have people who are just curious about the system like the "investigator" on my case, doing an investigative internship, with little to no supervision, from what I could tell, from professionals in the investigative field. And that is what public defenders are using as "investigators" to compete with police departments' investigators who do that for a living. . . .

Handling Too Many Cases

There is a Washington State law that requires counties and cities to pass legal standards on caseloads for their public defenders. The State Bar Association says the point of that enacted legislation was to institutionalize minimum *Constitutional* standards in public defense that currently did not exist across the state. Cowlitz County public defense attorneys, a neighboring county to King County, is cited as having a caseload [6.5] times what the state Bar Association has recommended. And . . . "in 1982, the King County Bar Indigent Defense Services Task Force developed a 300 case per attorney, per year guideline. This led to the Council passing a 1989 City Council Budget Intent Statement establishing a 380 case per-attorney, per-year limit. This bill reaffirms the caseload standards established in the City Council's 1989 Budget Intent Statement. Specifically, this bill states that City agreements with indigent public defense service providers shall require caseloads no higher than 380 cases per-attorney per-year. . . ." We have now the Bar Association, the Seattle City Council, the public defender organizations themselves, a [Washington] Supreme Court judge, *The Seattle Times*, *The Seattle Weekly*, and more, echoing that these services the public defenders are providing are inadequate. Yet every day more poor folks are locked up, due to what we all acknowledge is inadequate representation. It is sickening.

Strike to Raise Awareness of the Problem

There is legal precedent for public defenders to go on strike right now. First, they have Constitutional precedent. Most of the agencies involved echo that this erosion of public defense funding and services is an erosion of integrity to the entire judicial system. There is *indeed* a Constitutional right to fair representation and that right is being squelched currently due to inadequate public defender budgets. Secondly, in Seattle, the public defenders could go on strike right now due to the violation of the City Council's resolutions on maximum attorney caseloads per year, as they affect clients' Constitutional rights. It appears from where I sit, that these limits are violated in *every* county with a significant population, that contracts public defenders across the state. From Cowlitz to King Counties. It is time that the public defenders quit pretending they are giving a service they are not. And it is time they quit blaming others. If they cannot do their jobs, they need to admit it. Rather than doing half assed jobs where people go to jail as the payment for that half assed job. There are laws being violated by the state, city and county, from what I can tell, regarding these messes of public defender organizations used by the state.

I feel the only conscionable thing for public defenders to do is to go on strike, and to burst the myth of equal representation. Is it fair that the poor pay in jails for this mess? No, it is not. Seriously, public defenders need to go on strike. And demand a legitimate way to provide equitable legal services to the poor. But they should not continue to provide questionable legal services, yelling at clients under stress. They should stop now, and fight for the rights of the poor. Beginning with a right to fair and equal representation. Everyone from *The Seattle Times* to the Seattle City Council to the Washington State Bar Association publicly admits this problem exists. So how long are the poor going to be wrongly incarcerated for these crimes by attorneys and the state? How many families broken, how many criminals created, due to the lack of proper defense by public defenders? How long is this going to continue on? Public defenders have a DUTY to go on strike, is my take on this.

> "A defendant may well expect that the individual who is prosecuting the case against him will be partial, biased, and antagonistic. But the individual should not have to expect such prejudice from the judge."

Judges Are Failing to Safeguard the Rights of Poor Defendants

Richard Klein

In the following viewpoint, Richard Klein argues that many impoverished defendants in criminal court are coerced into plea bargaining for their alleged offenses. Klein blames defense counsel for inadequately researching a client's guilt, but he also faults judges for enticing defendants to accept plea bargains merely to speed cases through the overburdened courts. Klein asserts that judges need to remain impartial if the justice system is to function for all Americans. Richard Klein is a professor of law at Touro Law Center in Central Islip, New York.

Richard Klein, "Judicial Misconduct in Criminal Cases: It's Not Just the Counsel Who May Be Ineffective and Unprofessional," *Ohio State Journal of Criminal Law*, vol. 4, no. 195, 2006, pp. 195–198, 201–211, 213. Copyright © 2006 Ohio State University Moritz College of Law. Reproduced by permission.

As you read, consider the following questions:

1. In Klein's view, why is it common for prosecutors and police to overcharge defendants in criminal cases?

2. What are some of the threats and coercions judges have used to get defendants or their counsel to accept plea bargains, as Klein relates?

3. As Klein reiterates, what is the very first Canon of the American Bar Association Model Code of Judicial Conduct?

When evaluating the success or failure of the Supreme Court's decision in *Gideon v. Wainwright* in ensuring the effective assistance of counsel, the focus has often been on the poor quality of representation provided to indigents due to the inadequate funding of public defender or legal aid programs. This article will focus on the role of the trial judge, in particular the failure of trial courts to act to ensure that the constitutional guarantees to the effective assistance of counsel and to a fair trial are indeed honored.

The vast majority of criminal prosecutions throughout the country result in the defendant entering a plea of guilty. The Supreme Court, in *Brady v. United States*, has upheld the constitutionality of the plea bargaining process, and in *Santobello v. New York*, recognized that plea bargaining is an indispensable aspect of the criminal justice system. The process of plea bargaining is regulated by the Federal Rules of Criminal Procedure, the American Bar Association (ABA) Standards Relating to the Administration of Justice, the Uniform Rules of Criminal Procedure, and the Model Code of Pre-Arraignment Procedure.

Judicial involvement in the plea bargaining process in state courts can range from virtually non-existent to extremely controlling. It is in the high caseload, urban areas where judicial participation in the process is typically most marked, and most problematic. Administrative pressures prompt judges to move the court calendar by encouraging defendants to enter guilty pleas and thereby dispose of cases. As the New York State Court of Appeals bluntly stated in *People v. Selikoff*, the policy of the trial court which was directed at attaining guilty pleas was "acutely essential to relieve court calendar congestion. . . . In budget-starved urban criminal courts, the negotiated plea literally staves off collapse of the law enforcement system."

Plea Bargains Reduce Caseloads

It has long been the case in our urban criminal courts that "the need simply to dispose of cases has overshadowed everything else. . . ." The Supreme Court, in *Santobello v. New York*, one of its earliest decisions upholding plea bargaining, observed that "[i]f every criminal charge were subjected to a full-scale trial, the States and the Federal Government would need to multiply by many times the number of judges and court facilities." Plea bargaining is relied upon by public defenders not because it is always in their clients' best interest, but rather because it has become "a necessary technique to deal with an overwhelming caseload." It is not an overstatement to say that the utilization of plea bargaining has become critical to the very survival of many defender organizations. Indeed, the primary rationale for the formation of public defender offices as the mode in which governments chose to meet their obligations under *Gideon*, has been that it is a cheap method for representing as many defendants as possible in the shortest amount of time.

To be sure, the pressures and the needs of defenders to manage their caseloads can cause defenders to devote an insufficient amount of time to the representation of each of their clients. Inadequate preparation and investigation of the case as well as the failure to engage in thorough and effective communication with the client are perhaps the most egregious abuses. Even the most competent of attorneys simply will not be able to render the effective assistance of counsel if the lack of preparation has prevented counsel from uncovering readily available information that may well have yielded a more favorable plea bargain, a more effective cross-examination of a key trial witness, or a more lenient sentence were the defendant to be convicted at trial. Courts have long acknowledged that "effective assistance refers not only to forensic skills but to painstaking investigation in preparation for trial." The Ninth Circuit, in *Brubaker v. Dickson,* has gone as far as to conclude that the failure of counsel to investigate, research, and prepare is equivalent to no representation at all. . . .

Ensuring a Proper Defense

Professional standards clearly indicate that any decision to plead guilty and not risk trial is one that the defendant, and not counsel, must make. It is mandatory that the defendant's attorney, therefore, devote time with the defendant communicating what counsel's investigation has revealed regarding the strength of the prosecutor's case and the applicable issues of law, and advising his client of the possible results of the various options open to him. As the Supreme Court noted in *Tomkins v. Missouri,* informed and knowledgeable advice from counsel is required in order to overcome a client's ignorance or bewilderment.

The judge should ensure that the defense counsel is informed prior to the entry of any plea of any exculpatory material of which the prosecutor is aware. Both the ABA Model Rules of Professional Conduct as well as the ABA Standards for Criminal Justice require the prosecutor to make early and timely disclosure of exculpatory information. The standards, like all ABA approved standards, may be taking on more significance as of late due to two recent Supreme Court cases which do support the use of performance guidelines to review the quality of counsel's representation. In *Wiggins v. Smith,* the ABA Guidelines for the Appointment and Performance of

Defense Counsel in Death Penalty Cases were used to conclude that counsel's limited investigation for mitigating evidence indicated failure to provide effective representation. In *Williams v. Taylor*, the Court cited the ABA Standards for Criminal Justice to show that counsel's failure to seek available evidence, which could have assisted the defense, constituted ineffective assistance of counsel. . . .

It is indeed the obligation of the trial court to ensure that the adversary system is truly functioning. Our adversary system is based on the assumption that *both* sides have the opportunity to discover evidence that may be not only material as to the defendant's guilt or innocence but also to the determination of an appropriate sentence. The police and prosecutor may frequently over-charge the defendant in order to commence the plea bargaining process with additional leverage. How can defense counsel similarly engage in "posturing," or even calling the "bluff," unless counsel has had the opportunity to investigate the alleged criminal act?

Yet it is common for defense counsel in our large urban courts to offer a guilty plea on behalf of their client within minutes of having first met the defendant. The response of the trial court ought to be clear. The ABA Standards for Criminal Justice relating to "Pleas of Guilty" instruct the judge that "the court should not accept the plea where it appears the defendant has not had the effective assistance of counsel." And, in case more specific elaboration was required, the Commentary to the Standard states: "Because it is seldom possible to engage in effective negotiations minutes before the defendant is called upon to plead . . . a reasonable interval should elapse between assignment of counsel and the pleading stage."

Avoiding a Quick Guilty Plea

Judges may exploit the fact that there is a warm body with a J.D. [law] degree that is standing next to the defendant at the time that the plea is formally being entered; the "presence" of counsel may be used by the court to infer the "assistance" of counsel. However, the very reason that counsel is required is to avoid just the type of perfunctory process that so commonly occurs. In *Argersinger v. Hamlin*, the Supreme Court required the assistance of counsel due to the precise concern that were there *not* to be counsel appointed for indigent defendants, the heavy volume of cases in our criminal courts "may create an obsession for speedy dispositions, regardless of the fairness of the result." The Supreme Court's mandate in *Sheppard v. Maxwell* was clear: "[T]rial courts must take strong measures to ensure that the balance is never weighed against the accused."

Some appellate courts have appropriately created almost a presumption that when a guilty plea quickly follows the lawyer's initial consultation with the defendant, there has been either neglect by counsel or that the plea was entered due to pressures of time which precluded full preparation of any defense. Such a presumption may indeed be appropriate. Counsel's recommendation that his client plead guilty is often not the result of evaluating the available options after having conducted a thorough investigation of the relevant facts and law. To the contrary, the guilty plea may well be the *mechanism* for relieving counsel of the need to prepare the case. The caseload of the attorney may be so great that in order for him to "process" all of his cases, many of his clients simply *must* plead guilty. Yet a plea entered by a defendant because he knew that his lawyer was not then, and may never be, prepared and ready for trial, certainly is not a "voluntary" one on the part of the defendant. . . .

Judicial Complicity in Quick Pleas

Courts not only readily accept pleas where counsel has failed to provide effective representation, but the judges themselves may often inappropriately attempt to pressure an unwilling defendant to enter a plea. Judges are, to be sure, not immune from the caseload pressures that have permeated our criminal courts. Even the Supreme Court has taken note that "crowded calendars throughout the Nation impose a constant pressure on our judges to finish the business at hand." And when a plea is taken at the first arraignment of the defendant, typically the only information that is available about the crime the defendant has allegedly committed is from the police report. The judge is, however, professionally required to "be careful to allow sufficient time" for the defense to "properly prepare their case."

If a case on the judge's calendar has been called for judicial consideration of the matter and the prosecutor and defense counsel inform the judge that there is agreement on a plea, then the court typically does little. In the vast majority of those instances, the court will be told the D.A. [district attorney] recommendation for the sentence for the crime for which the defendant is to plead guilty, and the judge will agree to impose that sentence. But the judge properly has the responsibility for ensuring that the prosecutor is performing professionally and appropriately. Unlike any other attorney, the prosecutor has an ethical obligation extending beyond just the representation of his "client"; the prosecutor's responsibility encompasses the duty to seek justice and to "guard the rights of the accused as well as to enforce the rights of the public." The court is obligated to protect defendants from prosecutorial misconduct. The district attorney, like defense counsel, is an "officer of the court" and the court ought not abuse of what typically is very extensive prosecutorial discretion. The ABA Standards for Criminal Justice reflect the possibility that "personal ideological, or political beliefs . . ." of prosecutors might improperly influence a prosecutor's conduct as might the "desire for personal achievement, or for personal or political success. . . ."

But what if there is no "bargain" agreed upon? Judges may well just take things into their own hands. Since it is typically

"'How Do You Plead' Is Just a Legal Phrase," cartoon by Dave Carpenter. Cartoon Stock.com.

the defendant who the judge perceives to be the recalcitrant party, it is the defendant who becomes the object of the judge's attempt to "get rid of" the case. But what tools does the court have? One approach is to let the defendant know that if the defendant fails to enter a guilty plea on that day, the judge will never again impose such a "favorable" sentence. Take, for example, the judge sitting in the Supreme Court of New York State who told counsel who was standing next to the defendant: "Now the offer in this case, Mr. Barry, *for today only* is three to six which he [the defendant] obviously is not obligated to accept." The judge made it clear that if the defendant were to refuse the offered plea and go to trial, the judge would make sure that the defendant would be sentenced to the maximum time of incarceration permitted by law. The defendant continued in his refusal to plead guilty and responded to the judge: "I'm 19 years old, your Honor. That is Terrible. That's Terrible." The defendant then turned toward his mother who sat weeping in the courtroom and told her, "Mom, I can't do it," and jumped to his death out the window of the sixteenth floor courtroom.

The above mentioned case received press coverage because of the defendant's suicide, and not because of the coercive tactics employed by the judge. Comments such as "this is a one-time-offer", "for today only", and "I'll make sure you get sentenced to the max if you don't plead guilty now" are all too frequent to warrant newspaper headlines. There was no media coverage at all, for instance, when a juvenile court judge in Georgia stated: "I tell the minor, I will up the sentence if you take it to trial, because you could have pleaded and saved us all this trouble." Such threats certainly can overcome one's free will and can lead many individuals to simply agree to what is being demanded of them.

Threats and Other Unethical Persuasion Tactics

At times, the court directs the defense counsel to relay the message of the advisability of pleading guilty to the defendant. In *Commonwealth v. Longval,* the judge told counsel that "I strongly suggest that you ask your client to consider a plea, because, if the jury returns a verdict of guilty, I might be disposed to impose a substantial prison sentence. You know I am capable of doing that. . . ." And judges are not reluctant to deliver on their threats, and to make sure the defendant has learned his lesson. The judge, in *People v. Moriarity*, told the defendant upon being sentenced after a trial:

> If you'd have come in here, as you should have done in the first instance, to save the State the trouble of calling a jury, I would probably have sentenced you, as I indicated to you I would have sentenced you, to one to life in the penitentiary. *It will cost you nine years additional,* because the sentence now is ten to life in the penitentiary.

Any actual "negotiation" between a judge and a defendant appearing before that judge is extraordinarily difficult due to the clearly unequal power of the two parties. Even when there is no actual *intention* on the part of the judge to coerce the defendant to plead guilty, the *impact* of the judicial posturing will be of crucial significance. It is a given in any understanding of a true "negotiation" that there need be relatively comparable positions of power on each side. The judge, however, who is in the all-powerful position to imprison the defendant, is all-mighty when contrasted to an individual who is desperately seeking the most lenient sentence from the court.

The very first Canon of the American Bar Association Model Code of Judicial Conduct emphasizes the need for judges to act with integrity and impartiality so that the public will have confidence in the judiciary. The Supreme Court has mandated that the lower courts "must ever be concerned with preserving the integrity of the judicial process." Our criminal courts are perhaps the part of our justice system that is most visible to the public, and since the vast majority of criminal prosecutions result in guilty pleas, the ethical conduct of the judiciary in the plea bargaining process is of critical import. Even the "appearance of impropriety" must be avoided, and the Commentary to Canon I of the Code instructs that violating the Code "does injury to the system of government under law." The very first paragraph of the Preamble to the Code describes judicial office as a "public trust" where the judge is a "highly visible symbol of government."

Poor Defendants Often Confront an Antagonistic Court

One person to whom the judge certainly is visible is the defendant. A defendant may well expect that the individual who is *prosecuting* the case against him will be partial, biased, and antagonistic. But the individual should not have to expect such prejudice from the judge. However, how else is the defendant to interpret the judge's "one time, for today only" offer? And since so many minorities appear in our criminal courts as the accused and as family of the accused, might not those individuals believe that it is because of their ethnicity or color that the court appears to be so unconcerned with the rights of the defendant? Add to this, the attorney who has barely met the defendant and has engaged in no investigation, yet is aggressively promoting the prosecutor or judge's plea offer, and it is no wonder that the perception of indigents accused of crime is that the criminal justice system is stacked against them.

The American Bar Association was fully cognizant of the need to establish ethical standards in relationship to the plea bargaining process. Chapter 14 of the Standards for Criminal Justice is titled "Pleas of Guilty" and was recently revised to *delete* previous provisions which had permitted the judge to act as a "moderator" if the prosecution and defense counsel sought the court's assistance in arriving at a plea bargain. The most recent edition provides that a "judge should not through word or demeanor, either directly or indirectly, communicate to the defendant or defense counsel that a plea agreement should be accepted or that a guilty plea should be entered." The Commentary to this Standard emphasizes that "direct judicial involvement in plea discussions with the parties tends to be coercive and should not be allowed."

Our system of federalism requires that the state courts protect an individual's rights under the Constitution, and the state courts are to be the "primary guarantors of constitutional rights." Virtually every state requires that a judge upon assuming office take an oath to "support, protect and defend" the U.S. Constitution. The Supreme Court, in *Boykin v. Alabama*, concluded that even subtle threats from the judge concerning what might occur were the defendant to reject a proposed plea bargain, voids any subsequent plea. In *Glasser v. United States* the Court declared that "[u]pon the trial judge rests the duty of seeing that the trial is conducted with solicitude for the essential rights of the accused." The Court used even stronger language in *Lakeside v. Oregon* when it stated that "[i]t is the judge, not counsel, who has the ultimate responsibility for the conduct of a fair and lawful trial." The ABA has designated similar obligations for the trial judge in its Standards for Criminal Justice: Special Functions of the Trial Judge. The very first of the enumerated "Basic Duties" charges the judge with the responsibility for safeguarding the rights of the accused. The language of the Standard continues with what one could well interpret to be a caveat for the judges not to act as they so often do in regard to plea bargaining: "The trial judge should require that every proceeding before him or her be conducted with *unhurried and quiet dignity. . . .*" Another section of the Standards instructs the judge to treat the defendant with "professional respect, courtesy, and fairness." Judges are to "carefully avoid any words or actions that could undermine the dignity of the proceedings."

Jeopardizing Judicial Impartiality and Neutrality

Judicial pressuring of defendants to enter guilty pleas may violate judicial codes of conduct in two other regards. Judges are instructed to "give each case individual treatment, and the judge's decisions should be based on the particular facts of that case." Yet the judge who at arraignment, or at any time prior to defense counsel having had the opportunity to investigate the allegations of his client's criminal conduct, concludes what the plea and sentence should be, is not providing individualized justice. Too often the judge's all-too-hurried assessment of a case gives the impression that our criminal justice system operates in a mechanical manner. The American Bar Association Committee on Legal Aid and Indigent Defendants recently conducted extensive hearings across the country involving experts detailing the workings of our system for representing indigent defendants. The Committee's final report concluded that judges, in their haste to get guilty pleas, "accept and sometimes even encourage waivers of counsel that are not knowing, voluntary, intelligent, and on the record."

Perhaps most significantly, the judge who threatens the defendant with a harsher future sentence if the defendant does not plead guilty but chooses to go to trial, is not acting in the required neutral, impartial manner. The Special Functions of a Trial Judge inform judges that they "should not demonstrate even a *hint* of partiality." In *Ohio v. Filchock*, the Ohio Court of Appeals strongly condemned such judicial involvement. "It stretches the appearance of neutrality past the breaking point for a trial court to usurp the role of the prosecutor by formulating and proposing a plea bargain, and neither the State nor the Federal Constitutions will countenance such a practice." . . .

The dilemma is a clear one: in the vast majority of pleas, the defendant has been told by his own counsel, or by the prosecutor, or by the judge, that if he chooses to go to trial he will serve a longer period of incarceration than he would if he were to enter a plea of guilty. How is that not pressure? Coercion is especially a problem when the judge, who is in the clear position to impose sentence after trial, is involved in the attempt to "persuade" the defendant to plea guilty. When the judge tells the defendant that if he chooses to go to trial he will be sentenced to the maximum sentence authorized by law, that judge is clearly able to carry out that threat. As the South Carolina Supreme Court articulated in *State v. Cross*, "a plea induced by the influence of the judge cannot be said to have been voluntarily entered."

> *"Presuming innocence doesn't mean everybody is innocent; it means authorities must err on the side of your rights as an American citizen."*

Circumventing Police "Knock and Announce" Rules Violates Civil Rights

Radley Balko

In the following viewpoint, Radley Balko contends that rules of police procedure—such as the "knock and announce" rule and the exclusionary rule—are implemented to protect citizens' rights from unlawful and undignified police search and seizure raids. Balko insists that judicial rulings that threaten these rules grant excessive police powers at the expense of civil liberties. He favors keeping these rules in place to check aggressive police policies and procedures. Radley Balko, a libertarian, is an editor at Reason *magazine.*

As you read, consider the following questions:

1. As Balko relates, how long should law enforcement wait before entering a suspect's residence once they have knocked and announced their presence?

Radley Balko, "Hard Knocks with No-Knock: Why Is It Unreasonable to Announce and Wait?" *Reason Online*, June 20, 2006. Copyright © 2006 by Reason Foundation, 3415 S. Sepulveda Blvd., Suite 400, Los Angeles, CA 90034, www.reason.com. Reproduced by permission.

2. Why does Balko argue that constitutionality is not the "full measure" of an American citizen's rights?

3. In what way is part of the "knock and announce" rule about civilian and law enforcement safety?

For regular viewers of *COPS*, the real surprise in [the June 2006] U.S. Supreme Court decision in *Hudson v. Michigan*, which gives police officers greater leeway to conduct "no-knock" raids on residences, must have been that police failure to knock was an issue at all. Anybody who's seen the paramilitary searches and seizures that highlight the long-running police reality show (usually with a deadpan subtitle describing the action: "6:00 a.m., warrant served") might presume that police officers are *never* expected to honor the domestic peace of the people whose homes they're invading. The front door is bashed in with a battering ram, a squad of armed and armored officers enters the building, and only then do the shouting and announcing of police authority begin.

Last week, a 5-4 majority led by Justice Antonin Scalia ruled that violation of the "knock-and-announce" rule—a custom by which police serving a warrant knock on the suspect's door and wait some decent period of time (which in a previous case had been defined as 15 to 20 seconds)—does not require suppression of evidence found in a search. In the case, police searching for drugs and firearms at the home of suspect Booker T. Hudson announced themselves outside Hudson's home, did not knock, and failed to wait more than a few seconds before breaking down his door. They found drugs and a gun as described in the warrant, and the issue at hand was whether the failure to knock and wait was enough to invoke the "exclusionary rule," barring evidence obtained in an unconstitutional fashion.

Forces Hostile to the Exclusionary Rule

Scalia argues, and supporters of his decision agree, that there is no constitutional issue involved in the no-knock entry. In a

Booker T. Hudson's Defense Lawyer Asserts the Importance of "Knock and Announce"

Mr. David A. Moran: As this case illustrates, sometimes officers believe that it is to their advantage to perform a no-knock entry, or to fail to comply with the knock-and-announce requirement. And that is why—

Justice [Sandra Day] O'Connor: Why?

Mr. Moran: Well, Officer Good apparently thought that his safety would be better served he if disregarded the knock-and-announce requirement; and so, he candidly testified, at the evidentiary hearing, that it's essentially his policy, in drug cases, to go in without a—without performing the necessary knock-and-announce. And that was 1 year after the—this Court's decision in Richards, saying that there is no per-se exclusion of drug cases from the knock-and-announce requirement.

But that brings me to the second reason why courts have almost universally, until the Stevens case in 1999, held that suppression of evidence is necessary, and that is deterrence; because, without the suppression of evidence, there is very little chance that the officers will be deterred from routinely violating the knock-and-announce requirement, from adopting a sort of personal violation of the requirement.

Oral arguments before the U.S. Supreme Court in
Hudson v. Michigan, January 9, 2006.

glib editorial preemptively mocking "civil libertarians, especially those on the left," the *New York Sun* notes that the knock and announce rule is not written into the Fourth Amendment, or any other part of the U.S. Constitution. Instead, it is an English common-law practice dating back to the Middle

Ages. (It has been part of federal statutory law since 1917.) The George Washington University law professor Orin Kerr finds no conflict between Scalia's alleged "originalism" and his *Hudson* decision.

A survey of Scalia's legal record supports the suspicion that the judge is essentially hostile to the exclusionary rule, and may wish to eliminate it in all cases. Thus, the most interesting piece of writing on the *Hudson* case is neither Scalia's decision nor Justice Stephen Breyer's dissent, but the separate concurring decision by Justice Anthony Kennedy, which identifies a pattern of knock-and-announce violations as a cause for "grave concern," and supports the exclusionary rule as a remedy for other civil rights violations:

> [T]he knock-and-announce requirement protects rights and expectations linked to ancient principles in our constitutional order. . . . The Court's decision should not be interpreted as suggesting that violations of the requirement are trivial or beyond the law's concern. . . . [T]he continued operation of the exclusionary rule, as settled and defined by our precedents, is not in doubt. Today's decision determines only that in the specific context of the knock-and-announce requirement, a violation is not sufficiently related to the later discovery of evidence to justify suppression.

Scalia and Kennedy agree that the exclusionary rule is not a preferred means of assuring the right to privacy. In one flight of fancy, Scalia argues that "increasing evidence that police forces across the United States take the constitutional rights of citizens seriously" and the rise of civil rights litigation make civil court, rather than suppression of evidence, the proper avenue for challenging improper search procedures. Yale University law professor (and former Breyer clerk) Akhil Reed Amar agrees, arguing that the exclusionary rule protects the guilty rather than the innocent.

Authorities Should Err on the Side of Citizens' Rights

Does any of this make sense? If you presume that constitutionality is the full measure of your rights as an American citizen and a human being, maybe. But preserving the idea that American citizens are entitled to some dignity is about more than ruling out whatever wasn't specifically mentioned by the founding fathers. The idea that everybody is entitled to the presumption of innocence isn't mentioned anywhere in the Constitution either, but this concept underlies a range of customs and common law practices (most of which are also absent from the text of the Constitution) that have long been recognized as part of individual liberty. Presuming innocence doesn't mean everybody is innocent; it means authorities must err on the side of your rights as an American citizen.

Far be it from me to question Scalia's familiarity with the receiving end of police power, but when I look around, I see increasingly militarized police forces, where even beat cops have traded in spiffy suits and big shoes for jumpsuits and combat boots, and even the city of Sparks, Nevada has its own SWAT team. Scalia is confident that these are *not* people accustomed to viewing all civilians as potential enemies to be suppressed. But confidence in police training and professionalism is a thin hook on which to hang your right to be secure in your own home. Maybe the natural tendency to abuse power can be reined in by the mere threat of civil suits (most of which will inevitably be filed, as the lawyer C.T. Rossi notes in a colorful attack on the *Hudson* decision, by people in jail). I'd be more confident with a remedy that has some actual power.

Violence Begets Violence

Ironically, part of the impetus for the no-knock raid is the safety of police and civilians. There's a certain logic to that: A quick and efficient raid, in which the power of the police is immediately established and no resistance is possible, would seem like the quickest means of assuring domestic tranquility. But what happens when a citizen with a legally purchased handgun reacts to a home invasion, by people who have not knocked and are less than prompt in identifying themselves as police officers, in the most reasonable manner available—by shooting one of the invaders? The Mississippian Cory Maye is famously sitting on death row for shooting a cop who entered the bedroom of Maye's 18-month-old daughter during a no-knock raid of which Maye was not even the target. But Officer Ron Jones, by all accounts an excellent cop and standup guy, is dead. This case is not directly applicable, but the principle is the same: A violent home invasion increases the likelihood that somebody will get hurt, and the Supreme Court ought to proceed with caution before raising the likelihood of an event like that. We can take a charitable view and assume that Scalia and the high court majority are committed to reducing the amount of violence in America. But the best way to avoid a fight is not to start it.

"What makes the exclusionary rule so absurd is that it only protects people who are guilty of crimes."

The Exclusionary Rule Should Be Abolished

William Tucker

In the following viewpoint, William Tucker claims that the exclusionary rule is impractical and obsolete. Tucker argues that the exclusionary rule—which makes evidence found at a criminal suspect's home inadmissible in court if warranted searches are not properly executed—has been subverted by defense lawyers to get guilty clients off on minor procedural technicalities. Tucker hopes that a 2006 U.S. Supreme Court case, in which evidence found at a suspect's home was deemed admissible even though the police did not observe the required "knock and announce" procedure, will lead to the ultimate demise of the exclusionary rule. William Tucker is a journalist and the author of Vigilante: The Backlash Against Crime in America.

As you read, consider the following questions:

1. What was Alan Dershowitz's experience with the exclusionary rule, according to Tucker?

2. In Tucker's view, how can the exclusionary rule be subverted by judges?

3. Why does the author believe the "good faith exemption" is not enough to counter the abuses of the exclusionary rule?

In June [2006], the Supreme Court decided that Detroit police did not violate the Fourth Amendment rights of a drug dealer named Booker Hudson when they entered his home in August 1998 only five seconds after announcing their presence at his door. Hudson's lawyers argued that—although he had a loaded gun hidden in the couch next to him—police should have waited to enter for at least 20 seconds after knocking. The four dissenting justices in *Hudson v. Michigan* complained that the decision repealed a "knock and announce" rule that has been part of common law since the 13th century. Newspapers around the country echoed their lament.

Justice [Antonin] Scalia, writing the majority opinion, took aim at a rule of more recent vintage—the "exclusionary rule," enshrined by the Supreme Court only a generation ago, which holds that evidence must be excluded from trial if it has been obtained improperly. Dismissing key evidence on such a minor point as the number of seconds police wait at the door is the equivalent of giving the defendant a "get-out-of-jail-free card," wrote Scalia. The suppression of evidence should be "our last resort, not our first impulse."

Unfortunately, Justice Anthony Kennedy, who otherwise sided with the majority, did not endorse Scalia's rejection of the exclusionary rule. In a separate opinion, Kennedy called this rule "settled" and "not in doubt," but held that in this particular case the police did not overstep. Scalia's frontal assault on the exclusionary rule, though, now has the support of four justices. Before long, this judge-invented rule that redefined American law enforcement over the past half-century may reach the end of its long run.

The Mapp Case Extends the Exclusionary Rule

Its origins were certainly humble. On May 23, 1957, three Cleveland police officers came to the door of Dollree Mapp, who was suspected of harboring a suspect in a bombing case. (The bomb had gone off on the front porch of Don King's house—a warning to the future boxing promoter from rivals in the numbers racket.) Mapp called her lawyer, who told her not to allow the police to enter without a warrant.

The officers departed. Three hours later they returned with reinforcements, waving a piece of paper in front of her face and saying it was a warrant (whether it was remains in dispute). Mapp grabbed the paper and stuffed it in her dress. The police wrestled it back and put her in handcuffs. Her lawyer arrived but was not allowed to speak to her or enter the house. For the next few hours, police ransacked Mapp's home but didn't find their fugitive. In the basement, however, they did discover a suitcase that Mapp said belonged to a former tenant. Inside were four pamphlets, a couple of photographs, and a pencil doodling alleged to be obscene. Mapp was convicted of possession of pornographic material and sentenced to two to seven years in prison.

When Dollree Mapp's case came before the Supreme Court in 1961, search and seizure was not even the issue. Her conviction was appealed as a challenge to Ohio's strict pornography laws, and that was the subject of oral arguments. But President [John F.] Kennedy had just elevated his secretary of labor Arthur Goldberg to the bench to replace Felix Frankfurter, and for the first time the liberal faction led by Chief Justice Earl Warren had a majority. Without any preliminaries, the new majority seized on *Mapp v. Ohio* as an opportunity to do something it had contemplated a long time—extend the federal exclusionary rule on search and seizure to state criminal cases.

The Fourth Amendment to the Constitution reads as follows:

> The right of the people to be secure in their person, houses, papers, and effects, against unreasonable searches and seizures, shall not be violated, and no Warrants shall issue, but upon probable cause, supported by Oath or affirmation, and particularly describing the place to be searched, and the persons or things to be seized.

Until the 20th century, however, the Bill of Rights was interpreted as applying only to the federal government, not the states. This limited the scope of the Fourth Amendment, since most criminal investigations are conducted at the state and local level.

Thwarting Justice in the Name of Technicalities

The exclusionary rule was adopted for federal cases in a 1914 decision, *Weeks v. United States.* Fremont Weeks had been convicted of participating in a lottery through the mails, based on evidence seized from his Kansas City home without a warrant. Investigators had borrowed a key from a neighbor and searched his house, seizing evidence and other property. Weeks sued to have his property returned and the evidence excluded from the case. The Supreme Court, breaking with common law tradition, ruled in his favor. The "exclusionary rule" was promulgated as a remedy to deter violations of the Fourth Amendment. Benjamin Cardozo, then a New York state judge and soon to be on the Supreme Court, spotted the flaw right away: "The criminal goes free because the constable has blundered," he famously wrote. . . .

Over the next four decades, federal agents skirted the new rule by having state and local police gather evidence, handing it over in what became known as the "silver platter doctrine." While the FBI was circumscribed, state and local police forces were unrestrained by the Fourth Amendment. And so the Supreme Court decided to crack down. By a 5-to-4 vote, *Mapp v. Ohio* applied both the Fourth Amendment and the exclusionary rule to the states. Law enforcement has never been the same.

Mapp was the first of the Warren Court decisions that introduced the phrase "overturned on technicalities" into our language. *Miranda v. Arizona*, governing criminal confessions, is better known for introducing the phrase "you have the right to remain silent" and excluding numerous seemingly authentic confessions. But the exclusionary rule has had a greater effect on policing. Even today, many a criminal will confess to a crime to "get it off his chest." Even if he later thinks better of it, and claims he was coerced, the jury will usually be allowed to hear the confession and sort out the truth.

Mapp, however, involves physical evidence. Murder weapons, drug caches, even dead bodies turned up in police searches can be excluded from a case forever. In such instances, prosecution becomes impossible. Before *Mapp*, the "fundamental fairness" of a trial was viewed as the ultimate standard for deciding procedural issues. Since the decision, the courts have become endlessly bogged down in technicalities— such as how many seconds the police must wait before entering a home after knocking.

Overturning Guilty Charges

One of the first people to recognize this profound difference was Alan Dershowitz, who was clerking for Justice Goldberg when *Mapp* was decided. In his book *The Best Defense* (1983), Dershowitz recounts how as a defense attorney he learned to "put the state on trial" so that the conduct of the police, rather than the criminal, becomes the focus of the trial. Candidly admitting that nearly all his clients were guilty, Dershowitz told how he was able to spring numerous clients by arguing the minutiae of searches and seizures. His greatest triumph came in 1984, when he got a reversal of the conviction of socialite Claus von Bülow for the attempted murder of his wife. The family of Sunny von Bülow, who was left in a coma from an insulin overdose, had hired a private detective to search their home, uncovering a "black bag" containing hypodermic needles and other incriminating evidence. Dershowitz successfully argued that Rhode Island police should have obtained a warrant in order to accept evidence from the private detective. Without the evidence, von Bülow was acquitted at a second trial.

In the early years of the *Mapp* era, countless search warrants were overturned because of a misspelled name, a faulty street address, or transposed license plate numbers. In New Hampshire, a child murderer was freed because his wife had allowed police to search the house without his permission. "Evidentiary hearings" became the standard opening round of any criminal prosecution, and countless cases collapsed when technical violations by the police made key evidence inadmissible. A particular favorite of defense lawyers was the Fourth Amendment phrase "describing the place to be searched, and the persons or things to be seized." What constitutes an accurate "description" of evidence? Such a question could occupy philosophy students for whole semesters. If the warrant specifies a 9mm Smith & Wesson and the gun turns out to be a .357 Magnum, is it admissible? Police over time learned ways to fudge such details, but the result was constant hair-splitting.

Making the Rule a Tool of Judicial Bias

At worst, the exclusionary rule could become a simple excuse for judges to impose their will. In the 1970s and '80s, for example, the California Supreme Court under Chief Justice Rose Bird, openly hostile to capital punishment, overturned dozens of death penalty convictions. With metronomic regularity, the court would rule that a warrant had not sufficiently "described the place to be searched and persons or things to be seized." One notorious 1985 case finally led to the removal from the

The Exclusionary Rule Is Not Rooted in Common Law or the Fourth Amendment

Given that the exclusionary rule was announced over a hundred years after the Fourth Amendment was ratified, it is no surprise that the rule is not at all rooted in the actual language of the Fourth Amendment. The Fourth Amendment prohibits unreasonable searches and seizures. It says nothing about the exclusion of evidence that results from such seizures. It says nothing about the appropriate remedy for violations of the Fourth Amendment. The Supreme Court itself recognized this a few years after *Weeks* [*v. United States*], in *Olmstead v. United States*: "The striking outcome of the *Weeks* case and those which followed it was the sweeping declaration that the Fourth Amendment, *although not referring to or limiting the use of evidence in courts*, really forbade its introduction if obtained by government officers through a violation of the Amendment."

Even after the Supreme Court in *Weeks* reversed the common law rule that illegal evidence is not inadmissible, the Court still did not apply the exclusionary rule to civil trials, in which evidence discovered by legal and illegal searches alike continued to be admissible.

Nor did the Court initially apply the rule to states. Originally, the exclusionary rule applied only in cases involving the federal government, because the Fourth Amendment restriction on unreasonable searches and seizures applied only to federal and not to state officers. The separate states were free to adopt their own rules of evidence. . . . Most of the states rejected the exclusionary rule and continued to allow both civil and criminal courts to consider all probative evidence.

Patrick Tinsley and N. Stephan Kinsella, "In Defense of Evidence: Against the Exclusionary Rule and Against Libertarian Centralism," LewRockwell.com, November 1, 2003. www.lewrockwell.com

court of Bird and two colleagues by disgusted California voters. It involved Dr. Theodore Frank, a convicted child molester who had tortured and murdered a two-year-old girl. In the warrant, police had specified that they would search for "writings which could relate to the death of [the girl] and would indicate either participation and/or an interest in that death by Theodore Frank." What they discovered was a diary in which Frank confessed his fetishes. ("I want to give pain to these little children. I want to harm them.") The writings were read to the jury at the penalty phase, and Frank received a death sentence. Upon review, the Bird court ruled the warrant had been "overbroad," mere "boilerplate" that allowed police to "rummage" through Frank's possessions. They overturned the death sentence.

In 1984, an egregious Massachusetts case arrived before the Supreme Court. The bound and burnt body of a 25-year-old woman named Sandra Boulware had been found in a vacant lot in Boston. Her boyfriend, 45-year-old Osborne Sheppard, was implicated. Police obtained a warrant to search his apartment. Among other things, the warrant specified "a woman's jacket that has been described as black-gray (charcoal), any possessions of Sandra D. Boulware, similar type wire and rope that match those on the body of Sandra D. Boulware. . . . A blunt instrument that might have been used on the victim, men's or women's clothing that may have blood" on them, and so on. What they found was "a pair of bloodstained boots, bloodstains on the concrete floor, a woman's earring with bloodstains on it, a bloodstained envelope, a pair of men's jockey shorts and women's leotards with blood on them, three types of wire, and a woman's hairpiece, subsequently identified as the victim's." The Massachusetts Supreme Court threw out the conviction on the grounds that the warrant had not adequately described the "things to be seized."

Good Faith and Probable Cause

The Supreme Court finally put an end to this nonsense, carving out a "good faith exemption" to the exclusionary rule. If the police thought they were acting in good faith in conducting the search, then the evidence could be admitted. But of course this vague rule only opened up more opportunity for semantics. Whose "good faith" was involved? The police or the judge who issued the warrant? What constitutes "good faith"? That was for future courts to debate.

Meanwhile, defense attorneys moved on to new territory. The phrase of choice became "probable cause." Yes, a warrant might have been issued in good faith, and yes, the warrant might sufficiently describe the persons or things to be seized. But was there "probable cause" for issuing it?

Here's a good example. In the 1971 Academy Award-winning movie *The French Connection*, New York City drug detective "Popeye" Doyle and his partner see a small-time mobster celebrating with a party of friends at the Copacabana [nightclub]. "Something doesn't look right," he says, and they decide to follow the party home. They stake out the residence and eventually uncover the biggest drug shipment ever to reach New York City—a true story.

Such an investigation would be blatantly unconstitutional under today's standards, and all the evidence would likely be thrown out. Police cannot stake out a person's home, even a mobster's, because "something doesn't look right." They cannot follow hunches or investigate because a person "looks suspicious." For the most part, they must have evidence that a crime is being committed. When they seek a warrant, they must have specific, detailed knowledge of what they expect to find.

Of course, this philosophy of policing finally came home to roost in August 2001, when Minnesota FBI agents arrested Zacarias Moussaoui, an alien with an expired visa who had aroused the suspicion of flight school instructors in Minneapolis because he wanted to learn to fly a commercial jet without having any interest in how to take off or land. Dutifully following established procedures, the Minneapolis agents applied to Washington for a search warrant to look into his computer. FBI lawyers there turned down the request. There was no "probable cause" for investigating any further. All they had was a suspicious guy with an expired visa taking flight lessons. After forty years of playing Russian roulette with the American public, the criminal justice system finally hit a loaded chamber.

Protecting the Guilty

What makes the exclusionary rule so absurd is that it only protects people who are guilty of crimes. If the police come to your house, knock down your door, ransack your home, throw all your belongings in the street, and find no incriminating evidence, then the exclusionary rule offers you no compensation whatsoever. Only if evidence turns up that shows you to be guilty of something are you rewarded.

In pointing out how dated the exclusionary rule has become, Justice Scalia noted both the "increasing professionalism of police forces" and the ease with which aggrieved citizens can now pursue other remedies against the police for the violation of their rights. "Citizens whose Fourth Amendment rights were violated by federal officers could not bring suit until 10 years after *Mapp*," Scalia noted. Since then, "Congress has authorized attorney's fees for civil-rights plaintiffs. . . . The number of public-interest law firms and lawyers who specialize in civil-rights grievances has greatly expanded. . . . [E]xtant deterrences against [Fourth amendment violations] are . . . incomparably greater than the factors deterring warrantless entries when *Mapp* was decided. Resort to the massive remedy of suppressing evidence of guilt is unjustified."

After 45 years, the misbegotten practice of freeing the criminal because the constable has blundered may finally be about to come to an end.

Periodical Bibliography

The following articles have been selected to supplement the diverse views presented in this chapter.

Amy Bach	"Justice on the Cheap," *Nation*, May 21, 2001.
William Baldwin	"Put a Price on Your Liberties," *Forbes*, July 8, 2002.
Guido Calabresi	"The Exclusionary Rule," *Harvard Journal of Law & Public Policy*, Winter 2003.
J. Spencer Clark	"*Hudson v. Michigan*: 'Knock-and-Announce'—An Outdated Rule?" *BYU Journal of Public Law*, Winter 2007.
Mark A. Godsey	"Reformulating the Miranda Warnings in Light of Contemporary Law and Understandings," *Minnesota Law Review*, April 2006.
Arye Rattner, Hagit Turjeman, and Gideon Fishman	"Public versus Private Defense: Can Money Buy Justice?" *Journal of Criminal Justice*, March–April 2008.
Warren Richey	"A Defendant's Right to Confront Accusers: How Far Does It Extend?" *Christian Science Monitor*, April 22, 2008.
James S. Robbins	"Habeas Corpus Not Needed," *USA Today*, September 25, 2006.
Gerald J. Russello	"Prisoner's Dilemma," *American Conservative*, December 18, 2006.
James P. Terry	"Habeas Corpus and the Detention of Enemy Combatants in the War on Terror," *JFQ: Joint Force Quarterly*, Issue 48, 2008.

For Further Discussion

Chapter 1

1. Stanley S. Arkin advocates creating a magisterial review board to assess evidence to determine if prosecutors should pursue charges before a grand jury. Arkin hopes that such a review board would check the controlling power most prosecutors have in shaping the outcome of grand jury decisions and ensure that cases expected to generate "public agitation and uncertainty" are necessary if evidence is weak. Do you believe Arkin's added safeguard is worthwhile? Why or why not? What might be the pros and cons of creating a magisterial review board?

2. After reading the viewpoints by Jesselyn McCurdy and Steve Chapman, explain whether you think law enforcement engages in racial profiling. Defend your view with quotes from the articles and any personal anecdotes you may have. Also, explain whether you think racial profiling might ever be a useful tool in law enforcement.

Chapter 2

1. James Q. Wilson argues that the high incarceration rate in the United States is correlated with decreased rates of crime. On the other hand, Howard N. Snyder and Jeanne B. Stinchcomb contend that high incarceration rates do not necessarily result in decreased crime. Whose argument do you find more convincing, and why? Use specific evidence and quotes from the texts to support your answer.

2. According to Douglas B. Marlowe, prison reentry programs have often failed to aid prisoners in returning to society because they do not offer the inmates focused rehabilitation, and typically allow them to neglect the re-

quired follow-up without consequence once they are released. Based on this critique, do you think the reentry program presented by Mark A. Nadler would significantly reduce recidivism? What benefits and disadvantages does Nadler's program have? Do you think that Marlowe's critique of prison reentry programs is useful in developing new programs? Explain your answer.

3. The First Amendment to the Constitution states, "Congress shall make no law respecting an establishment of religion, or prohibiting the free exercise thereof." This clause is used to justify the restricting of religious practices in public institutions such as schools, prisons, and courthouses. Still, many prisons are offering faith-based rehabilitation programs to aid prisoners in transitioning back to productive lives in society. John D. Hewitt argues that these programs help individuals and thus should be supported by the government and the public. Lawrence T. Jablecki on the other hand maintains that because these programs violate the First Amendment, they should not be sponsored by public funds or the government. Based on these arguments, and your own interpretation and understanding of the First Amendment, do faith-based prison programs violate the Constitution? Why or why not?

Chapter 3

1. Debate over the death penalty is perennial. Supporters like David B. Muhlhausen tout its ability to deter criminals from committing violent crimes, while detractors such as Amnesty International contend that its deterrent effect is minimal and that capital punishment is nothing more than state-sponsored murder. Which of these arguments do you find more convincing? Are there additional issues that you consider when forming your opinion on the death penalty? What are they? How does you personal background and belief system impact your viewpoint?

2. Crack cocaine sentencing laws were formulated in the mid-1980s to combat the growing epidemic of crack cocaine use and the crimes committed in association with the drug's use and sale. Penalties for possessing a small amount of the drug were harsh—some said unfairly so. These sentencing laws were recently reformed, and even those who were convicted before the reform now have the opportunity to appeal their sentences. Gretchen C.F. Shappert argues that retroactive reform of the sentences is a mistake. Marc Mauer contends it finally gives those convicted an opportunity to receive fair sentences. Do you agree with Shappert who believes that retroactive reform will leave criminal justice "deprived of much of its deterrent effect," or do you agree with Mauer that the sentences were disproportionately long in the first place and retroactive enforcement will finally hand down fair sentences? Which author's cost-benefit analysis of retroactive enforcement is more convincing? Use specific examples from the texts to support your opinion.

Chapter 4

1. The debate over the right of war detainees to know the charges against them and to contest their indefinite detainment is hotly contested. After reviewing the viewpoints by Aziz Huq and Andrew C. McCarthy, explain whether you believe detainees captured in the United States' "war on terror" have the right of habeas corpus. Explain why you do or do not agree with President George W. Bush that it is within executive purview to detain captives without trial as long as hostilities remain.

2. Kirsten Anderberg suggests that public defenders are failing in their duties to defend poor litigants adequately because public defenders are overworked and over-stressed, leading to poor relations with clients. Richard Klein argues that judges are compounding this problem by leading

poor litigants to accept plea bargains in order to speed cases through the system. Given that these problems exist, how would you remedy the legal aid and trial system to ensure that low-income defendants are protected?

3. William Tucker believes that the exclusionary rule and "knock and announce" rule have become tools of defense lawyers looking for a means to get guilty clients off the hook. Do you agree with Tucker? Do the exclusionary rule and the "knock and announce" rule seem to protect those who are guilty of crimes through technicalities of procedure? Explain your answer.

Organizations to Contact

The editors have compiled the following list of organizations concerned with the issues debated in this book. The descriptions are derived from materials provided by the organizations. All have publications or information available for interested readers. The list was compiled on the date of publication of the present volume; the information provided here may change. Be aware that many organizations take several weeks or longer to respond to inquiries, so allow as much time as possible.

American Bar Association (ABA)
740 15th St. NW, Washington, DC   20005-1019
(202) 662-1000
e-mail: crimjustice@abanet.org
Web site: www.abanet.org

The American Bar Association is a voluntary membership organization for professionals within the legal field that provides law school accreditation and works to promote justice, excellence of those within the legal profession, and respect for the law. The Criminal Justice Section of the ABA is dedicated to maintaining the integrity of criminal justice law and providing information on the state of the criminal justice system in the United States. *Criminal Justice* is the quarterly magazine of this section of the ABA, which also publishes an annual report on the state of the criminal justice system.

American Civil Liberties Union (ACLU)
125 Broad St., 18th Floor, New York, NY   10004
(212) 549-2500
e-mail: aclu@alcu.org
Web site: www.aclu.org

The American Civil Liberties Union works to ensure that there are no infringements upon the rights guaranteed to all U.S. citizens by the Declaration of Independence and the

Constitution. Criminal justice is a main focus of the organization. The ACLU files cases and petitions to challenge what it sees as unjust laws, rulings, and sentencing, and the organization also works to ensure that the rights of traditionally underrepresented individuals such as minorities, the poor, and young people, are protected within the criminal justice system. The ACLU's Web site provides handbooks, project and public policy reports, pamphlets, and other publications.

American Enterprise Institute (AEI)

1150 17th St. NW, Washington, DC   20036
(202) 862-5800 • fax: (202) 862-7177
Web site: www.aei.org

The American Enterprise Institute is a conservative public policy institute that promotes the values of limited government, private enterprise, individual liberty, and a vigilant defense and foreign policy. Articles, books, lectures, and conferences published and sponsored by the organization have addressed issues within the criminal justice system such as the implementation of the death penalty, the impact of high incarceration rates, and how to address the imprisonment and rights of terrorist suspects. The *American* is the bimonthly magazine of the AEI; articles from this publication and additional commentary can be accessed on the AEI Web site.

Amnesty International

5 Penn Plaza, New York, NY   10001
(212) 807-8400 • fax: (212) 627-1451
e-mail: aimember@aiusa.org
Web site: www.amnestyusa.org

Amnesty International operates through a network of national offices worldwide, all with the goal of ensuring that human rights, as guaranteed in the Universal Declaration of Human Rights, are observed and respected globally. Over two million members worldwide share in the work. Amnesty opposes the death penalty as a form of punishment and advocates for its abolishment. Additionally, the organization intervenes in what it sees as abuses of the criminal justice system and mishandling of specific criminal cases. Publications about Amnesty International's views on criminal justice issues as well as information about current activities can be found on its Web site.

Cato Institute
1000 Massachusetts Ave. NW, Washington, DC   20001
(202) 842-0200 • fax: (202) 842-3490
e-mail: cato@cato.org
Web site: www.cato.org

A libertarian, public policy research institute, Cato is committed to promoting limited government, individual liberties, and a free-market economy. With regard to the criminal justice system, Cato maintains that many behaviors have become over-criminalized and the punishments for many crimes have become too severe. The Cato policy report "Overextending the Criminal Law" outlines the stance of the institute. Additional articles and commentary on criminal justice in America can be found in the quarterly *Regulation*, the bimonthly *Cato Policy Report*, and the periodic *Cato Journal*.

Families Against Mandatory Minimums (FAMM)
1612 K St. NW, Suite 700, Washington, DC   20006
(202) 822-6700 • fax: (202) 822-6704
e-mail: famm@famm.org
Web site: www.famm.org

Founded in 1991, Families Against Mandatory Minimums works to educate the government and the public about what it sees as the unfairness and negative impact of mandatory minimum sentencing. The organization is trying to change the stringent sentencing policies that guarantee offenders long, minimum sentences that, it argues, do not always fit their criminal backgrounds or crimes. Through advocacy campaigns on both the state and local level designed to put a human face on an abstract issue, FAMM has been able to affect sentencing. Reports and papers outlining the history of mandatory minimums and their impact, as well as information on FAMM's current activities, are available on the organization's Web site.

Heritage Foundation

214 Massachusetts Ave. NE, Washington, DC   20002-4999
(202) 546-4400 • fax: (202) 546-8328
e-mail: info@heritage.org
Web site: www.heritage.org

The Heritage Foundation is a conservative public policy organization dedicated to promoting policies based on free enterprise, limited government, individual freedom, and a strong national defense. Heritage supports the use of the death penalty and maintains that a strong and aggressive local police force is a leading factor in reducing crime when used in combination with policies that incarcerate violent criminals to remove them from society. The organization also runs the Web site *overcriminalized.com*, which reports on what it sees as unprecedented criminalization of social and economic behaviors. Articles on crime-related issues can be found on the organization's Web site.

National Center on Institutions and Alternatives (NCIA)

7222 Ambassador Rd., Baltimore, MD   21244
(410) 265-1490 • fax: (410) 597-9656
Web site: www.ncianet.org

NCIA has been working since 1977 to reform the human service and correctional systems so that those who come into contact with them can break the destructive cycle of committing crimes and imprisonment. The organization seeks to aid individuals who are convicted of crimes in receiving reduced sentences, and then to follow up with these individuals and help them to adjust to life in prison and eventually obtain parole if they are eligible. The center's Web site provides information on current activities and publications about the importance of aiding those who are in prison.

Sentencing Project

514 10th St. NW, Suite 1000, Washington, DC   20004
(202) 628-0871 • fax: (202) 628-1091

e-mail: staff@sentencingproject.org
Web site: www.sentencingproject.org

The Sentencing Project seeks to reform current sentencing laws and practices, and advocates for decreased reliance on incarceration as a form of punishment. This organization seeks to change the way that Americans view crime and punishment by providing facts about the negative impact incarceration has on individuals and, as a result, the country as a whole. Focuses include racial disparity in sentencing, drug policy, and women in the justice system. Publications on these issues and others are available on the Sentencing Project's Web site.

U.S. Department of Justice (USDOJ)
950 Pennsylvania Ave. NW, Washington, DC   20530-0001
(202) 514-2000
e-mail: AskDOJ@usdoj.gov
Web site: www.usdoj.gov

The USDOJ is the office of the U.S. government charged with upholding the laws of the United States in order to protect the country as a whole, as well as all American citizens. Additionally, the department provides federal guidance for the prevention and control of crime to ensure that all Americans receive fair and impartial judgments and sentencing in accordance with the Constitution. Articles about current DOJ activities can be found on its Web site along with links to other DOJ agencies such as the Civil Rights Division, the Drug Enforcement Administration, and the Federal Bureau of Prisons.

United States Sentencing Commission (USSC)
One Columbus Circle NE, Washington, DC   20002-8002
(202) 502-4500
e-mail: pubaffairs@ussc.gov
Web site: www.ussc.gov

The USSC was established in 1984 by the Sentencing Reform Act provisions within the Comprehensive Crime Control Act of that same year. It is an idependent agency in the judicial branch of the government, responsible for setting sentencing policies and practices for federal courts, serving as an advisor to Congress and the executive branch in the development of crime policy, and acting as an information clearinghouse for the government and the public on issues relating to federal crime and sentencing. The ultimate goal of the agency is to provide fair and consistent sentencing for those who commit crimes within the United States. Reports and documents published by the organization are available on its Web site.

Bibliography of Books

Howard Ball — *Bush, the Detainees, and the Constitution: The Battle over Presidential Power in the War on Terror.* Lawrence: University of Kansas Press, 2007.

Hugo Adam Bedau and Paul G. Cassell — *Debating the Death Penalty: Should America Have Capital Punishment? The Experts on Both Sides Make Their Case.* New York: Oxford University Press, 2005.

Michael Braswell, Larry Miller, and Joycelyn Pollock — *Case Studies in Criminal Justice Ethics.* Long Grove, IL: Waveland, 2006.

Mark Costanzo — *Just Revenge: Costs and Consequences of the Death Penalty.* New York: St. Martin's Press, 1997.

Angela Y. Davis — *Are Prisons Obsolete?* New York: Open Media, 2003.

Kevin Davis — *Defending the Damned: Inside Chicago's Cook County Public Defender's Office.* New York: Atria, 2007.

Rolando V. del Carmen and Chad R. Trulson — *Juvenile Justice: The System, Process and Law.* Belmont, CA: Wadsworth, 2005.

Jack L. Goldsmith — *The Terror Presidency: Law and Judgment Inside the Bush Administration.* New York: Norton, 2007.

Tara Herivel and Paul Wright
Prison Nation: The Warehousing of America's Poor. New York: Routledge, 2002.

Steve Holbert and Lisa Rose
The Color of Guilt & Innocence: Racial Profiling and Police Practices in America. San Ramon, CA: Page Marque Press, 2004.

James A. Inciardi
Criminal Justice. New York: McGraw-Hill, 2006.

Eleanor Hannon Judah
Criminal Justice: Retribution vs. Restoration. New York: Routledge, 2004.

David Klinger
Into the Kill Zone: A Cop's Eye View of Deadly Force. San Francisco: Jossey-Bass, 2006.

Christian Parenti
Lockdown America: Police and Prisons in the Age of Crisis. New York: Verso, 2000.

Joycelyn M. Pollock
Ethical Dilemmas and Decisions in Criminal Justice. Belmont, CA: Wadsworth, 2006.

Jeffrey Reiman
The Rich Get Richer and the Poor Get Prison. Boston: Allyn & Bacon, 2007.

Anthony Thompson
Releasing Prisoners, Redeeming Communities: Reentry, Race, and Politics. New York: NYU Press, 2008.

Jeremy Travis
But They All Come Back: Facing the Challenges of Prisoner Reentry. Washington, DC: Urban Institute Press, 2005.

Samuel Walker and Charles M. Katz	*The Police in America.* New York: McGraw-Hill, 2007.
Samuel Walker, Cassia Spohn, and Miriam DeLone	*The Color of Justice: Race, Ethnicity, and Crime in America.* Belmont, CA: Wadsworth, 2006.
Brian L. Withrow	*Racial Profiling: From Rhetoric to Reason.* Upper Saddle River, NJ: Prentice Hall, 2005.

Index